# Top Time Management Tips

- **Spend a moment to plan each and every day.** Take a few minutes to jot down the few key things you need to achieve today.

- **Set a time limit.** You're more focused and less likely to get distracted if you don't have an open-ended time slot in your day for a particular task.

- **Write everything down.** You'll save time and be less stressed if you're not holding all those things you're trying to remember in your head.

- **Focus on important tasks.** Don't just focus on the urgent items.

- **Look at your longer-term goals.** Ask yourself how what you're doing each day fits in with your goals.

- **Do little and often.** Breaking tasks into chunks helps to prevent a build-up and is less overwhelming when you're only spending a few minutes on a task.

- **Take a break.** Doing so might seem counterintuitive, but if you try to cram too much into your day you end up stressed out and exhausted. Have regular breaks and you'll be more productive.

- **Don't do it all on your own.** Don't hesitate to ask for help when you need it. Chapter 11 provides tips on delegation.

- **Keep the balance.** Try not to spend all your waking hours at work – make time for home, family, and friends, and make sure you leave time to eat properly and exercise regularly. Chapters 15 and 16 have more information on taking time for yourself, family, and friends.

# Questions to Keep You Focused

Ask yourself these questions to help you keep focused on the task in hand and stop wasting time doing unnecessary tasks:

- Is what I'm doing right now helping me to achieve my goals or objectives?
- What is the best use of my time right now?
- Is the task urgent?
- Is it important?
- Will it enhance my life?

*For Dummies: Bestselling Book Series for Beginners*

# Time Management For Dummies®

Cheat Sheet

## Top Time-Saving Tips

This book is full to bursting with time-saving tips, but here's a snapshot of the best:

- ✔ Plan, plan, and plan (Chapter 4 can help).
- ✔ Have one diary for everything.
- ✔ Switch off your email alerts (Chapter 8 has more on dealing with emails).
- ✔ Use a timer when you're trying to complete a task.
- ✔ Schedule tasks in blocks of time.
- ✔ Carry a notebook with you to make lists and make sure you don't forget anything.

## A Quick Checklist for Dealing with Procrastination

When you get stuck and keep putting something off, ask yourself these questions to get you moving again:

- ✔ What are you putting off?
- ✔ What impact will not doing this task have?
- ✔ What's stopping you?
- ✔ What's the benefit of doing the task or not doing it?
- ✔ What can you do to make the first step?

Choose one of my procrastination-busting tips:

- ✔ **Take one step at a time.** Don't try to tackle big tasks all in one go; do one little bit at a time.
- ✔ **Do it now.** You've put something off for long enough – just take yourself by surprise and do it.
- ✔ **Get someone else to do it.** If you don't have the time or energy to do it yourself, delegate! (Chapter 11 helps you perfect the art of delegation.)

Turn to Chapter 2 for loads more on overcoming procrastination.

**For Dummies: Bestselling Book Series for Beginners**

# Time Management

FOR

# DUMMIES®

# Time Management
## FOR
# DUMMIES®

## by Clare Evans

John Wiley & Sons, Ltd

**Time Management For Dummies®**

Published by
**John Wiley & Sons, Ltd**
The Atrium
Southern Gate
Chichester
West Sussex
PO19 8SQ
England

E-mail (for orders and customer service enquires): cs-books@wiley.co.uk

Visit our Home Page on www.wiley.com

For general information on our other products and services, please contact our Customer Care Department within the U.S. at 800-762-2974, outside the U.S. at 317-572-3993, or fax 317-572-4002.

For technical support, please visit www.wiley.com/techsupport.

Wiley also publishes its books in a variety of electronic formats. Some content that appears in print may not be available in electronic books.

British Library Cataloguing in Publication Data: A catalogue record for this book is available from the British Library

ISBN: 978-0-470-77765-7 (PB)

Printed and bound in Great Britain by TJ International Ltd

10  9  8  7  6  5  4  3  2

WILEY

# About the Author

**Clare Evans** is a personal and business coach working with individuals and businesses to improve their time management, increase productivity, and create a better work life balance in these time-challenged times.

Clare worked in the corporate sector for a global company for many years. Managing IT projects and working with global teams, she understands the pressures today's working environment places on people's time and the difficulty of creating a better work–life balance.

Now running her own business, Clare coaches people one-to-one and runs workshops, seminars, and teleclasses on the subjects that challenge our time. She frequently writes and publishes articles for newsletters and magazines such as *Zest*, *Cosmopolitan*, and *New Woman* magazines, *Better Business Focus* (a monthly Internet magazine for business advisers), and *Financial Solutions* (the Personal Finance Society's magazine for financial advisers).

Everyone cares about the best use of their time. Clare specialises in enabling people to achieve what they want in ways that makes people master their use of precious time.

For additional information about time management, or to invite her to speak at your meeting or event, you can contact Clare at info@clareevans.co.uk. You can visit her website and sign up for her free newsletter at www.clareevans.co.uk.

# Author's Acknowledgements

My thanks to all the team at Wiley for pulling this book together. Wejdan Ismail for getting things started, Rachael Chilvers for her patience and encouragement throughout the process of writing, and the rest of the team at Wiley who edited, tweaked, and proofread.

Special thanks to Christine Brown, Stephen Cotterell, and Martin Bamford for their support and encouragement throughout the writing process. To friends and family who have checked in along the way to see how the writing was going.

Thank you to Rory Singer for the conversation that got me started on writing the initial outline for the book and for one of those synchronous moments.

My thanks to my many clients who have shared their challenges and questions over the past few years and given me the opportunity to use my skills and experience to make a difference to their lives. For all those who are always coming to me with their questions and challenges, it's been a pleasure to not only be able to answer them but to see the significant changes that some of them have made.

Last but not least, thanks to my parents, who have always been there and from whom I no doubt inherited most of my skills at organising my own time. To my Dad for being able to prove that it's possible to have organised 'chaos' and my Mum for just being organised and having a list for everything.

# Publisher's Acknowledgements

We're proud of this book; please send us your comments through our Dummies online registration form located at www.dummies.com/register/.

Some of the people who helped bring this book to market include the following:

*Acquisitions, Editorial, and Media Development*

**Project Editor:** Rachael Chilvers

**Development Editors:** Rachael Chilvers and Charlie Wilson

**Copy Editor:** Martin Key

**Proofreader:** Anne O'Rorke

**Commissioning Editor:** Wejdan Ismail

**Publisher:** Jason Dunne

**Executive Project Editor:** Daniel Mersey

**Cover Photos:** © Paul Hardy/Corbis

**Cartoons:** Rich Tennant (www.the5thwave.com)

*Composition Services*

**Project Coordinators:** Erin Smith, Lynsey Stanford

**Layout and Graphics:** Reuben W. Davis, Melissa K. Jester

**Indexer:** Claudia Bourbeau

**Brand Reviewer:** Zoë Wykes

# Contents at a Glance

# Table of Contents

# Introduction

*T*ime management is a bit of a misnomer. You can't actually manage time. Time just is. All you can hope to do is manage yourself and what you do with your time – that's my definition of *time management*.

This book provides you with tools, tips, and ideas to enable you to get control of your time, and find ways of managing yourself and others around you so that you can do more with the time that you have. Even if you don't think that you can ever be organised, you can always change something that makes a difference. It's surprising how something small – a new habit you adopt or a tip you take on board – can make a big difference.

In our modern 24-hour society there never seem to be enough hours in a day, as you face more and more demands at work and at home. Poor time management results in a loss of productivity and worse – increased stress and poor health. The good news is this book doesn't just show you how to be more organised, but also how to find more time for yourself: to relax, to spend time with family and friends, and to do something that busy, over-worked people often fail to fit in – have fun!

## About This Book

*Time Management For Dummies* is ideal for those of you who need to brush up your time management skills. Nearly every-one can do something to use their time more productively and avoid wasting time. This book can help.

The book is divided into easy-to-read sections that cover specific challenges with practical exercises along the way. I cover all manner of subjects – from tackling time-wasting to giving you the best time-saving strategies.

Although some of my advice may not be new, reading it again never hurts. A little bit more sinks in each time and repetition reinforces knowledge and skills.

# Conventions Used in This Book

To help you navigate through this book easily I use a few conventions:

- *Italics* are used for emphasis and to highlight new terms.
- **Bold-faced** text indicates keywords in numbered or bulleted lists.
- Monofont is used for web addresses, which direct you to further sources of information.
- Sidebars are the grey boxes that contain interesting information, anecdotes, or something fun relating to the chapter or section's topic.

# Foolish Assumptions

While writing this book I've made some assumptions about you and your knowledge of time management:

- You're perfectly capable of managing your time, like most of the people I work with; you just have some blocks around doing so.
- You recognise that you waste a lot of your time and you want to do something about it.
- You want some simple, straightforward advice, tips, and ideas on how you can be more organised.
- You fit into one of the following categories:
  - You've read quite a bit about time management already but want reminders of the key skills.
  - You're starting from scratch and want to know how best to organise your time.
  - Someone has mentioned or dropped a hint that you could benefit from improving your time management.

> ✔ You realise that you can't actually manage time, only
> yourself. It's just easier to phrase it that way.

# How This Book Is Organised

*Time Management For Dummies* is divided into six major
parts, each of which is divided into chapters that focus on key
topics relating to time management.

The great thing about *For Dummies* books is that you don't
have to read them all the way through. Each chapter is self-
contained, providing ideas, tips, and information on a different
issue. If you want to, you can simply turn to the area you need
to focus on – a chapter, a section, or even just a paragraph.
The table of contents and the index help pinpoint where to
find the info you need.

The following is a brief summary of what's in each section.

## Part 1: What Is Time Management?

This part begins with why it's important to manage your time
in an effective way and then helps you identify exactly where
all your time goes. If you've never done this before it may be
an interesting, eye-opening exercise, especially when you
realise just how much your time is worth. I then move on to
look at the things that get in the way of you getting on, and
give you plenty of strategies to help you get motivated. Finally,
I explore something that often leads to dithering and time
wasting – making decisions.

## Part II: Getting Your Time in Order

This part sets some of the ground rules and key strategies you
need to start using if you want to be more effective. Optimise
how you use your diary or calendar, and see how just a few
minutes' planning immediately increases the amount you get
done each day. Find ways to create an action list that actually

works, rather than a to-do list that comprises a never-ending list of things you need to do – if only you had the time. And discover how setting boundaries and saying no to people gives you more time for yourself.

## Part III: Organising the Work You Do

This part is about the nitty-gritty of managing your time, giving hands-on, practical tips that address the main areas that challenge people in their day-to-day life. Creating systems and processes to deal with each of these particular areas is important if you want to avoid being disorganised, overwhelmed, and totally stressed out. Avoid wasting time being distracted and interrupted, and find out how to make even better use of your time by doing less and getting someone else to do things for you.

## Part IV: Working from Home

Many people now work from home. Outside of the traditional office environment, home-working requires a different discipline and comes with unique challenges. This part shows you how to organise yourself, both in finding a work style that suits you and in getting to grips with the practical side of having a home office, so that you can work more comfortably and efficiently.

## Part V: Looking at the Bigger Picture

Although it's important to get as much as you can out of every day, including increased productivity, a income to live on, and efficiency at work, you mustn't forget why you're doing it. This part is all about finding time for the important things in your life – you, your family, and your friends. If you had more time, you'd probably spend it on being healthier. Don't let your health take a back seat just because you're too busy to exercise regularly, eat properly, or take time to relax. Read this part and you'll be able to reset your work–life balance.

## Part VI: The Part of Tens

This part includes lists of ten things that help you to save even more time. I give you ideas of things to do when you've got a few spare minutes, and tell you about ten gadgets that can save you time and effort.

# Icons Used in This Book

This book won't throw lots of questions at you, but it should certainly set you thinking. These icons highlight some of the points you may find most thought-provoking and useful:

This icon highlights something that's just a little bit different from a conventional tip.

This icon draws your attention to an important point to bear in mind.

I give really great time-busting tips with this icon. Think of it as a sort of turbo-boosting time tip – this icon shows you where you can really start to make the best use of your time.

This icon highlights tips and tricks that can help you manage your time more effectively.

If there's something you need to watch out for, then I use this icon. Ignoring this point can cost you time.

# Where to Go from Here

*Time Management For Dummies* is a reference book, designed to give you the most helpful information in an easy-to-read, user-friendly way.

You may decide to read through the book one chapter at a time, or if there's a particular issue you'd like to get started on right away then you can skip to the relevant chapter. You can dip in and out of the book as necessary, but I recommend reading through the first two chapters at some point because they're important for setting the scene and identifying your existing time habits.

However you read the book, and wherever you go from here, the most important thing is to do something with the information, tips, and advice in this book. Remember, little changes add up to big differences.

# Part I
# What Is Time Management?

"Of course you're tired— if you're going to be saving the world several times a day, you _must_ plan your time better."

## In this part . . .

*I* take a look at what your poor time management is really costing you, and the benefits of managing your time more effectively. One of the biggest challenges people have is putting things off, so in this part you find out what you can do about tackling procrastination.

# Chapter 1

# Replacing Bad Time Habits with Good Ones

*E*veryone has the same 24 hours in the day – you, me, the Queen, Sir Alan Sugar, and the person in your local shop. However, what you get out of those 24 hours depends entirely on how you spend them. Highly successful people use their time highly successfully. Now, you may not be aiming for 'highly successful' but, given that you're reading this book, you probably want to be more efficient and productive with your time.

'There simply isn't enough time in the day to get everything done,' I hear you cry. Contrary to popular belief, there is enough time. Most people's problem is that they try to do too much in the time available, or they don't organise and plan effectively, so they constantly waste time.

If your desk looks like a tip and you can never find anything, if you only ever get a piece of work done when a deadline is looming, and if you guzzle caffeine so that you can burn the midnight oil, then perhaps you need to look at how your current habits affect the way in which you manage your time – and then change some of those habits.

# Understanding the Importance of Time Management

Because you have only 24 hours in each and every day, making the best use of these hours makes good sense. Once those hours have gone you can't get them back, and you can't make more of them if you lose or waste them. They're a finite resource, which means that spending a little time brushing up your time management skills can transform your life in various ways.

## Increasing productivity

It's all too easy to get to the end of the day and wonder what you've actually achieved, even though you feel as though you haven't stopped all day. Many a time I've known people who say 'I've been really busy all day but what did I do?' I've done it myself. You're busy but not necessarily productive.

Managing your time means you're more effective. You get more done in less time, you focus on the important things and so your overall productivity increases.

For example, by managing your time better, you may be able to carve out an extra half-hour a day. Spend that half-hour on your most important project every day for a week and you'll be astonished at how you chip away at the work. Good time management now has a great long-term effect.

## Reducing stress

If I were to wave a magic wand and give you an extra hour in every day, what would you do? Usually when I ask this question, the most common responses are – sleep and exercise, or just time to relax. These responses go to show what kind of activities tend to get pushed to one side when time is short or when people try to cram too much into what's available and what's physically possible.

Poor time management leads to overload, frustration, lack of motivation, and poor self-esteem. The longer your poor time management continues, the more stressed, tired, and ill you become.

You get caught in a vicious circle. You never get time to catch up or get on top of things. You just keep doing things the same way because you don't know how to do them any differently, or you feel that you just don't have the time. Eventually, something has to give and too often it's your physical and emotional health that suffers.

Developing better time management skills can reduce your stress levels. You're then able to manage your workload better and take control of your life rather than feel your life is controlling you all the time.

## Achieving a happy work–life balance

The point of better time management is that you're able to do the things that are important to you and create balance in *all* areas of your life, not just at work. Many people who are over-worked, with too much work to do in those 24 hours, spend too much time doing just that – working.

Life isn't just about work. Work is a means to an end. Work provides you with the income to enable you to live the lifestyle you choose. Head to Chapter 14 for more information about how you can be more time-savvy when it comes to work and money.

As working hours increase and people work longer and longer, getting some balance between your work life and your personal life becomes very important. If you didn't have work, you'd still have your family, friends, and your health. Developing better time management skills means you stop neglecting yourself and your loved ones because you're 'too busy at work'. Chapters 15 and 16 have heaps of tips about taking time out for yourself and for your friends and family.

Managing your time effectively means you focus on what's important in the time you have available, so you make time for the essential things in life.

The chapters in Part V give you advice on how to keep things in perspective and maintain a better balance.

# Identifying How You Prefer to Work

Only you know how you work best, and whether your time habits are a hindrance or a help. One person's chaos is another person's order.

There's no right or wrong way of working:

- ✔ Some people like a lot of detail and create charts and lists to monitor their progress; others prefer to work with big ideas and leave the detail to others.
- ✔ Some people like writing lists; others hate them.
- ✔ Some people like working with pen and paper; others think the more technical gadgets they can have the better.
- ✔ Some people are naturally neat and tidy and love having a clear desk; others aren't and like to have everything out where they can see it.

Are you a left- or right-brained person? Well, obviously you're both but people have preferences for using one side of their brain than the other. The left side of the brain is more logical and analytical; the right side is more creative. A style of working that suits a more left-brained person won't always suit a more right-brained person. Both can be trained but it makes sense to work with your natural preferences. In this book I provide a variety of methods that you can pick and choose from to suit the way your brain works.

Although you can read all the time management books you like, you need to find and adapt what works best for you. Many people get put off because they read something that says they should work in a certain way or lay their desk out according to a particular plan or number all their files in a certain way. They throw their hands up in horror because that method just isn't them.

Whatever your natural style and preference, use your strength and natural abilities to organise and manage your time in a way that works best for you, otherwise you end up constantly paddling upstream or just getting frustrated.

## Becoming an expert in an hour a day

Just think what you could do if you set aside an hour in each and every day. Scientists discovered that to become a world-class expert takes 10,000 hours – so in only 10,000 days you could be an expert in something. Okay, it'll take you 27 years, but you're only spending an hour a day.

Even the most talented musician or artist began knowing nothing but they got to the peak of their field with practice. Set aside 5–10 hours a week and you can become at least pretty competent in your chosen field. Why not start to play an instrument, take up painting, or get stuck into a sport? Do something for yourself in those hours, and then enjoy the long-term rewards.

# *Setting Goals to Focus On*

Before you begin to look at ways to manage your time better, you need to know where you're going and why. You're more likely to be successful if you've created some specific goals to work towards.

If you don't know where you're going, how are you going to know when you get there? You wouldn't set out on a journey without looking at a map. If you're managing your time but you find that your time and effort isn't getting you closer to your goals, then what are you doing?

Ask yourself:

- ✔ What gets you out of bed in the morning?
- ✔ What is your big goal or dream?
- ✔ What do you want more of?
- ✔ What do you want less of?
- ✔ Where would you like to be in a year, two years, five years, ten years?

Make sure that your goals are your own and not someone else's goals or expectations (such as those of your parents).

You need to make your goals SMART, a useful acronym that means making them really clear and specific.

- ✔ **Specific:** Don't set a goal to 'do more exercise'. If you want to find time to get fit, set a goal to walk or run a specific distance, or exercise for thirty minutes, three times a week – complete a sponsored walk, or run a 10 kilometres race.

- ✔ **Measurable:** Make sure that you can measure your progress and know when you've achieved your goal. To exercise three times a week for thirty minutes is a measurable amount and you can track your progress each week.

- ✔ **Achievable:** Don't decide to run a marathon if it's *way* beyond your current skills and ability – you're just setting yourself up for failure. Think about the time, resources and skills available.

- ✔ **Relevant/Realistic:** Make sure that your goals fit with your bigger vision for your life or business. Stretch yourself but be realistic, otherwise you won't commit to it and you'll be easily de-motivated.

- ✔ **Time-bound:** Set an end-date for achieving your goal. This stops it drifting off into something indefinite and gives you a target to aim for.

Create a solid, underlying reason for achieving your goals. What benefits and impact is achieving them going to have on your life? Get really clear about what these goals mean to you and you're more likely to achieve them. Anything is possible.

Write down a few specific goals or your one BIG goal. Pin them up where you'll see them every day.

If you don't tell someone about your goal, you're answerable to no one but yourself and it's too easy to let yourself off the hook. Telling someone else about your goal helps to keep you motivated. Share goals so that you can keep each other on track. Find a partner, friend, colleague, mentor, or a coach to work with.

# Creating New Time Habits

The previous sections of this chapter help you understand how you use your time and set goals for what you want to achieve. Moving forward, though, involves letting go of some bad habits that are making you less efficient and productive.

Breaking a habit takes time. You've taken years to adopt the habits you have, but be aware that you can *un*-adopt them, especially if they're habits that don't serve you. Be prepared to give yourself time to develop new habits and don't expect to get the process right first time. Research shows you can change a habit in around thirty days (or about thirty occurrences), so stick with it.

## *Improving your planning*

How do you know what you're going to do today, this week, this month? Planning is a fundamental part of time management. Remember the saying, 'If you fail to plan, you plan to fail.'

Planning is critical if you're busy and even when you're not. Plan your year, your month, your week, and your day in advance. Don't just plan time for work – book time for yourself as well. Use the time management tools I explore in Chapter 3, and the action lists I explain in Chapter 4. Your plan isn't written in stone – it's adaptable and flexible; review your plans regularly to keep them relevant and up to date.

Always keep your goals in mind when planning (see the earlier section 'Setting Goals to Focus On' for more). Youstill have many tasks you need to complete each day but now youneed to focus on the important ones. You can ignore any actions that are likely to lead you off in the wrong direction or distract you. These actions won't get you where you want to be any quicker or more easily. You'll just waste your time and energy on them.

Spending just a few minutes planning each day really saves you time in the big picture. You won't waste time wondering what to do next, letting important tasks fall by the wayside, or feeling pressured by deadlines and a workload that threatens to swamp you. Plan your time and see what a difference it makes.

## *Managing your workload*

Sometimes, your workload can feel like a huge, unscalable mountain looming over you. But with a little organisation, you can break that mountain down to just a few gentle hills you need to get over or gradual steps to take you to the top.

Chapter 2 helps you get over the hurdles that prevent you from getting on with your work, and shows you how to split tasks into simple steps. Then Chapter 4 shows you how to prioritise your tasks so that you can tick them off steadily. And Part III offers a range of tips and ideas on how to handle specific elements of your work – from meetings and paperwork, to emails and phone calls.

## *Organising your time*

So you've planned out what you need to do, you've sorted the tasks or arranged them in some form of order, and now you need to actually organise your time to get them done. You need to take control of your own time and space and find a way of working with time and within time, in a way that works for you.

This book contains a wealth of ideas to help you better organise your time. For example, in Chapter 4, I discuss structuring your time effectively – from breaking it into manageable blocks, to introducing variety into your day. And, to help you stay focused, in Chapter 10 I look at handling and minimising distractions and interruptions.

A little organisation goes a long way. You need to get everything in place so that you can be a smooth time manager, a super efficient, highly organised person, a king or queen of productivity . . . (okay, maybe not, but it doesn't hurt to aim high!)

Sometimes doing nothing is the right thing to do. Part of the problem with time management is that you're expected to make use of every waking minute of every hour of every day and . . . well, you don't! It's perfectly okay to stop and just relax sometimes. Chapter 15 gives you more tips about freeing up your day for some me-time.

Find out which area of your life needs attention and focus on that area first and see how great your life can be.

One way to assess how you're doing and how balanced your life really is right now, is to try this exercise.

Draw a large circle on a piece of paper and divide it into eight sections. Label each section with the following titles or use your own to define all the different areas of your life (you may have more than eight).

- ✔ Money
- ✔ Career/Business
- ✔ Health
- ✔ Personal Growth
- ✔ Fun/Social Life
- ✔ Friends/Family
- ✔ Partner/Relationship
- ✔ Physical Environment

Now score each of the eight areas on a scale of one to ten. Ten means your life in this area is complete and can't possibly be improved. Zero means things can't be any worse.

If zero is the centre of the circle and ten is the outer edge, draw a line on each section to represent your score, as shown in Figure 1-1.

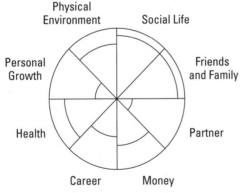

**Figure 1-1:** A filled-out wheel of life.

Most people find that their areas score between 4 and 8 with one or two areas scoring high (8 or more) and one or two scoring low (5 or less).

If any of these sections is seriously out of balance – 3 or less, you're probably tired, stressed, and unhappy with your life. Imagine this is the wheel on a bicycle. How bumpy would your ride be with an unbalanced wheel with bits missing?

The chapters in Part V show you ways to find time to improve these sections of your life to create a better balance.

# Chapter 2

# Getting On with the Task in Hand

. . . . . . . . . . . . . . . . . . . . . . . . . . . . . . . . . . . . . . .

## In This Chapter

▶ Looking at the consequences of procrastination

▶ Tackling what's holding you back

▶ Using different strategies to get moving

▶ Working on your decision-making

. . . . . . . . . . . . . . . . . . . . . . . . . . . . . . . . . . . . . . .

*P*art of changing any pattern of behaviour is to take a look at how you're currently behaving and what needs to change. The same thing applies to how you use your time. If you can identify where your inefficiencies creep in and when and where you're least productive, then you can start doing something about those particular areas and using your time more effectively.

The following sections contain exercises that help you get a clear picture of how you currently manage your time.

## Unmasking Your Bad Habits

The fact that you bought this book implies you may have an inkling that your time management skills aren't quite what they should be. But before you can get to grips with tackling the behaviour that's limiting your time, you need to work out just which bad habits you've fallen into.

Take a look at the following list and consider which habits apply to you:

- You're always late for meetings.
- You often work late just to keep on top of things.
- You often miss deadlines.
- Your filing tray is overflowing.
- You have a backlog of emails that you need to deal with.
- You never pay your bills on time.
- You're always taking on more work.
- You're always rushing round with never a moment to spare.
- Your family and friends hardly see you.
- You never have time for exercise and eating properly.
- You take more time off work than you used to.
- You waste time on low priority activities.

Recognise any of those habits? I'm sure that I've missed a few – can you add on any other time habits you have that you'd like to change?

## *Giving yourself a grilling*

The previous section helps you identify which bad habits may be affecting your time management. Now I ask you to take a step further, and really think about how you use your time.

Work your way through the following sections. Try to give honest answers – no one's grading your responses. This exercise is to help you really get a handle on what you need to change.

- How many hours a day do you spend on/at work?
- How much time each day do you spend on paperwork, emails, and phone calls?
- What proportion of your time do you spend in meetings?
- How much of your time is spent dealing with crises or urgent issues?

- ✔ Do you choose how to use your time, or do other people manage your time for you?

- ✔ How often do you get distracted or interrupted during the day?

- ✔ Do you put things off until the last minute?

- ✔ What are your biggest time wasters?

- ✔ Are you able to say 'No' to your colleagues/boss when they ask you to do something?

- ✔ How much time do you spend planning what you need to do?

- ✔ Do you have a to-do list that's out of control?

- ✔ When is your most/least productive time of day?

- ✔ How do you prioritise your tasks or do you deal with them as they come up?

- ✔ Do you have time for yourself, and your family and friends?

If you're beginning to realise that you're not going to win an award for Time Manager of the Year, don't despair. This book is all about helping you improve your current habits around managing your time, one step at a time.

## Recording your time

People often have a distorted view of how long things take. So the best way to get a clear picture of how you currently manage your time is to start making a note of exactly what you do, when, and for how long.

Spend the next week making a note of everything you do on a day-to-day basis. Make it as detailed as you like. You may want to apply your notes just to the hours you spend at work or you can extend them to cover the whole of your day. What time do you get up, how long does it take you to get ready in the morning, how long does it take you to get into work, how much time do you spend exercising, how long do you spend with friends and family, and so on? Write everything down and you'll have a better idea of where you're spending your time.

Table 2-1 shows a simple daily time log you can copy and adapt your needs. Remember, there are no right or wrong answers. At this stage you're just seeing where your time currently goes. Add as much detail as you need.

| Table 2-1 | Sample Daily Time Log |
|-----------|----------------------|
| *Time* | *Task* |
| 7.00 | Get up/shower/ breakfast |
| 8.00 | Leave for work |
| 8.30 | Arrive – check emails |
| 9.00 | Team meeting |
| 10.00 | Coffee break |
| 10.10 | Write report |
| 11.30 | Emails |
| 12.30 | Lunch |
| 13.15 | Phone call |
| 13.50 | Grab paperwork and leave for meeting |
| 14.00 | Project meeting |
| 15.10 | Email follow-ups |
| 15.30 | Project work |
| 16.00 | Phone calls |
| 16.20 | Project work |
| 17.00 | Emails |
| 17.30 | Leave work |
| 19.30 | Cinema and meal with friends |
| 11.30 | Bed |

# Thinking 80/20

The Italian economist Vilfredo Pareto came up with the Pareto Rule or Law as a mathematical formula to show the distribution of wealth. He found that 80 per cent of the wealth is owned by 20 per cent of the people – in every country.

This rule, known as the Pareto Principle, can be applied to many associations between cause and results – 80 per cent of the problems come from 20 per cent of the causes; 20 per cent of sales staff achieve 80 per cent of the sales; 80 per cent of your business comes from 20 per cent of your customers.

You can apply this principle to time management – 80 per cent of the results you achieve come from 20 per cent of the effort. To put it another way, if you took a list of 100 tasks, 20 of them (say, phone calls, emails, and meetings) would achieve 80 per cent of the results you want. The rest are less important tasks. That's not to say they're not worth doing, but remember to focus on the important 20 per cent first.

Instead of spending time on all 100 tasks, focus your effort on the 20 per cent of high value tasks and activities that can get you 80 per cent of the results. If you look at your task list, calls, and emails, you should have a good idea of which ones are likely to be more productive. If you're not sure, measure the results you get from your activity. Making one phone call may be more productive than sending twenty emails. One hour of effort on a key task can be more productive and achieve greater results than four hours spent on the 'wrong' task.

People spend a lot of time, money, and effort on things that don't get results or make us happy. Do more of what's important and what you enjoy and you can achieve 80 per cent of your results in 20 per cent of the time and with less energy.

You know when you're 'in the flow' and things seem easy – you achieve greater results for less effort!

At the end of the week, look at all your daily time logs and add up how much time you've spent on different types of tasks and activities such as:

- Breaks
- Emails
- Exercise

✔ Meetings

✔ Phone calls

✔ Socialising

✔ Writing

Now you've got a better idea of where you're spending your time each day. You can probably already see in a few obvious areas that you're not using your time very effectively; for example, times when you're interrupted or distracted, jumping from one type of task to the next. Perhaps you've noticed the things that you *don't* have time for – exercise, socialising, family.

## Breaking down your average day

What matters in time management is how much of the 24 hours in any given day you devote to each different task.

Breaking your day down into time segments can help you realise just how you're spending your time at present. Take an average work day, and estimate how many hours you spend on:

✔ Chores (shopping, cleaning, and so on)

✔ Personal activities (eating, washing, dressing, for example)

✔ Sleep

✔ Travel

✔ Work

After you add up the hours you spend on these various things, you know how much time you have left on average for yourself – to exercise, to socialise, and to relax.

For example, Sarah breaks down her average day as follows:

| Activity | Time spent (hours) |
| --- | --- |
| Chores | 1 |
| Personal | 1 |
| Sleep | 7 |

| Activity | Time spent (hours) |
|----------|--------------------|
| Work | 9 |
| Travel | 2 |
| **Total** | **20** |

Sarah discovers that in the average day, she has just four hours out of 24 as 'free time'. Not a lot, is it?

# Counting the Costs of Procrastination

Procrastination has got to be the number one time management problem that I spend much of my time dealing with. You leave something to the last minute – either because you've got so much to do that you just work on whatever is shouting the loudest, or because you keep putting tasks off until they *have* to be done. Like that tax return.

However efficient you may be in certain areas of your life, you undoubtedly put things off from time to time. But when procrastination is leading to stress and poor time management, you need to deal with your problem.

Putting something off may seem like an easy option, but what is the long-term impact? You just create more stress for yourself when you push everything up against a deadline or leave things to the last minute.

Here are some consequences of procrastination:

✔ **Finances:** In financial terms what is procrastination actually costing you? If you pay a bill late, you end up paying interest. If you don't submit your tax return on time, you pay a fine. If you don't get work to a client on time, you risk losing his business.

✔ **Opportunities:** How many opportunities are lost because you've put off making a decision or getting something done? Someone asks you to complete a report or provide some feedback but by the time you get round to doing it, she's asked someone else or gone ahead without you.

✔ **Time:** If you keep putting things off, sooner or later they're going to have to be done. You keep putting things off and before you know it you've run out of time and you end up stressing yourself out, working long hours, and potentially missing out on something you'd rather be doing. You waste time and energy procrastinating – worrying or feeling guilty about what you 'should' be doing when you could actually be doing it.

✔ **Wellbeing:** When you focus on less important tasks and ignore something of greater importance (in other words, you don't manage your time well), you worry about the task without actually doing anything about it. The more guilty you feel, the more distracted you become. Your sleep pattern, eating habits, and general stress levels suffer. Long-term stress can lead to illness and depression.

Completing a job that you've put off for ages feels pretty good. But the buzz and relief of finally getting the job done doesn't cancel out all the stress you put yourself through by putting the job off in the first place. Don't fall into the habit of thriving on that adrenalin rush at the end of a period of stress.

✔ **Workload:** If you leave tasks to the last minute you put more pressure on yourself. Instead of spreading your workload over an extended period of time, you end up cramming all those put-off or leftover tasks into a shorter and shorter time frame and just increase your workload.

# *Identifying Procrastinating Behaviour*

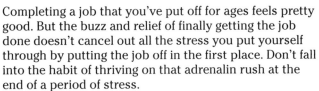

The first step to combating procrastination is to recognise when you're doing it. Signs that you're suffering from the procrastination lurgy include:

✔ Leaving tasks until the last minute when they become urgent or just can't be put off any longer.

✔ Pushing all thoughts of the task out of your mind for now – 'I'll worry about that tomorrow.'

✔ Hoping the task goes away, or that someone else does it for you.

✔ Making excuses for why you're not ready to begin the task – perhaps you don't have enough information.

✔ Ignoring more important tasks and busying yourself with easier, less urgent ones – how much housework do you do when you know that there's something more important you should be doing?

✔ Allowing interruptions to distract you from your main purpose, getting sidetracked, and taking long breaks.

Procrastination is a habit you can break. As with any habit, the first step to breaking free is realising that you're avoiding doing things in the first place. Then you can move on to working out why you procrastinate, and how to stop.

# What's Stopping You? Tackling the Roots of Resistance

We all have a tendency to put things off for various reasons – lack of motivation, skill, poor time management, fear, self-doubt, personal problems, distractions, perfectionism, to name a few.

Like any problem, you first need to address the cause, not the symptom. In this section, I look at some of the main causes of procrastination, and show you how to combat each.

## Challenging action-barring thoughts

Here are some common reasons why you may stick your head in the sand, ostrich-style, to avoid doing something, and how you can tackle these limiting thoughts:

✔ **Yawn! That job looks as dull as ditchwater.**

People do tasks that are more interesting, exciting, or that they feel more comfortable doing, in preference to the more difficult, mundane, or boring tasks, even though these tasks are important.

If something's important, think about why it's worth doing. How can you make a task more fun? Try setting a time limit to see how quickly you can do the task, reward yourself when you've done it, or get someone else to do it (turn to Chapter 11 to perfect the art of delegation).

✔ **I'm not waving, I'm drowning . . .**

You may procrastinate because you've taken on too much in the first place. Take a step back, be more realistic about what you can achieve, and organise your time to do both the important stuff and the fun stuff.

Chapter 4 give you more information about prioritising tasks.

✔ **I work best when I leave things to the last minute.** Sometimes a little pressure is good and yes, you often do your best work when you're up against a deadline but in reality you end up being stressed and burnt out.

Look at how you can plan your time better to avoid this happening as a matter of course. Make working last-minute the exception and not the way you always work.

✔ **What's the point, anyway?**

It's easier to put something off when you're not sure what to do next or there's no clear outcome. If you can't see the benefit then you're not going to be motivated to do it.

Face your fear or uncertainty and write down where the gaps are, and what the expected or desired outcome is. Look at how this task fits with your overall goals. Who else has the expertise or can provide advice on how to get this job done?

✔ **That job? Easy – I'll do it later.**

Easy tasks can create the most resistance – procrastination isn't always as a result of complexity. You might feel that a task is so easy you can do it later and you then just forget it or you keep putting it off.

If a job is that easy, do it now. If you really don't have time, add it to your list so at least you don't forget about it and set a time for 'later'. Set a time for when you're going to do it.

> ✔ **That job? Huge and horrible – I just can't face it now.**
>
> The longer you leave it, the harder it becomes. Usually by that time, it's become critical rather than just being important. Huge jobs are often less intimidating and more manageable if you break them down into smaller jobs. (Read the later section 'Breaking down tasks'.)

When the pain of not doing something becomes greater than the pain of doing it, resistance magically disappears. And more often than not, you find that the task you've been avoiding like the plague isn't so bad after all.

## Conquering fear that holds you back

Fear of failure can stop you from doing anything at all. If you don't do the task, you can't fail. If you've experienced failure in the past, no matter how long ago or even if it's unrelated to the current situation, it can have a powerful effect on stopping you from moving forward. Too often people think that it's not acceptable to fail, that failure is bad – no wonder we worry about getting things wrong.

The fear of actually doing something is usually far worse than the actual task itself, yet we still do it. Put off a task and it can start to develop almost ogre-like proportions and you waste precious time before you finally get round to doing it. You assume the worst when actually, when you get round to doing it – it's not as bad as you first thought. The more you think about it the worse it seems – and you slip into the trap of analysis, paralysis, and wasting even more time.

Here are some strategies for conquering your fear and dealing your procrastination:

> ✔ **Write down your fears:** Putting them down on paper helps you evaluate them calmly and logically. Are they real or imaginary?
>
> ✔ **Be brave:** Nothing that's really worth doing is going to be easy – challenge yourself and do something scary. The more often you do this, the more you expand your comfort

zone and the easier it is next time. Plan in time to tackle the scary tasks when you know that you're in the right frame of mind.

✓ **Let go of the inner critic:** Sometimes we're our own harshest critics and we set unrealistic expectations of what we 'should' be doing. If you tell yourself the outcome must be just right, first time, you can find yourself too scared to even try, because you inevitably fall short of your own super-high standards. Replace perfectionism with doing your best. Think of times when you've been successful.

✓ **Equip yourself:** If your fear comes from a lack of knowledge or ability, improve your skills and work out how to deal with the situation. Spend time developing new skills or acquiring knowledge.

✓ **Change the language:** Talk about a learning experience rather than a failure. So what if things don't work out as you expect? Your experience can help you next time. Remember, there's no such thing as failure – only feedback.

Making a mistake can be a powerful lesson. No one succeeds without making a few mistakes along the way. You can achieve so much more if you recognise that mistakes are okay.

# Getting Going Again

Whatever your reason for putting something off, the following sections offer strategies and techniques to help you shake yourself out of procrastination mode.

## Sorting out your priorities

Ask yourself the following questions:

✓ Is what I'm doing the most important, best use of my time right now?

Is this job really important or just a 'nice, fun thing to do'? Is there something more important that needs doing?

✓ Is what I'm doing moving me closer to, or further away from, where I want to be?

Make sure that the outcome of each task aligns with your goals, whether business or personal, otherwise you're wasting time and effort. Is there something more important that needs doing? Chapter 1 helps you determine your goals.

## Making effective plans

Planning is a great time management strategy and key to keeping focused and avoiding the temptation to put things off. If you know what you need to do and you set aside time to do it, you have no excuse to put it off.

However, the best-laid plans can change. Sometimes taking action and doing something is the best way to get yourself out of a rut or stop yourself wasting time by putting something off. Chapter 4 shows you how to organise your time and your tasks to get the most out of your day.

Plan time into your schedule in advance – don't leave things until the last minute. Spending just a few minutes each day planning makes a real difference to how productive you are for the rest of the day.

## Creating efficient systems

What tasks do you always tend to delay or put off? Putting systems in place for the tasks that commonly fall by the wayside makes life easier and removes the excuse for procrastination.

Here are some examples of systems and approaches you can use to more efficiently manage your time:

- Pay all your bills on direct debit.
- Organise paperwork as it comes in (see Chapter 7).
- File on a regular basis.
- Keep your work/living space clear and uncluttered, so you don't get distracted by other things that 'need doing'.
- Say no (see Chapter 5) when you don't have the capacity (or inclination) to do something.
- Embrace a 'little and often' attitude to avoid things building up.

Make yourself accountable. Tell a friend, colleague, or mentor (or coach) what you're going to do and you're more likely to get it done. If you tell someone else about what you need to do and when you're going to do it, not only are you more likely to achieve it but it keeps you motivated as well – plus, that person can help to keep you on track.

# Breaking down tasks

You've no doubt heard the phrase, 'How do you eat an elephant? One bite at a time.' Well, the same thing applies if you have a large overwhelming task that you're putting off. Break the task down into smaller more manageable tasks, so that firstly, it's not so overwhelming and secondly it's easier to do.

### Creating manageable chunks

Break a project down into smaller and smaller tasks until you have a series of basic steps.

For example, to put up a shelf, your steps may be as simple as these:

1. **Get the shelf, toolbox, and ladder.**
2. **Mark the shelf's position on the wall.**
3. **Drill holes.**
4. **Stuff fixing plugs in the holes.**
5. **Attach brackets to the wall with screws.**
6. **Put books on shelf.**

### Working through step by step

Once you've broken down a task into its multiple parts, you can take the parts one step at a time. Because now you don't have to do everything at once, the task seems much less daunting. Sometimes you can't see the whole path ahead or your end goals, just a few steps at a time, but as soon as you take those steps you can see where you need to go next.

Here's how to work through your small tasks effectively, always with the goal in mind of better managing your time:

✔ Break the task down into its multiple parts and create a list of steps to follow, using the example in the preceding section.

✔ Get everything ready that you need to complete the task – but don't use this task as a delaying tactic.

✔ Start with the first step (or choose a task to start on if there's no chronological order to the tasks). Focus wholly on this task and work through until you've finished.

✔ Finish one task before moving on to the next. Don't have too many tasks on the go at once. Stay focused.

✔ Take frequent breaks to keep your mind from getting distracted. If you're tired or lose focus your efficiency drops, so take a break for a few minutes and come back refreshed.

✔ Plan how long you intend to spend working, and then force yourself to stop after a set time. That way, the steps won't be too tiring or overwhelming.

✔ Stop where you can easily pick up next time. If you can, finish a step rather than abandoning one halfway.

## Taking it one boulder at a time

Setting little targets enables you to complete the distance more easily.

In Joe Simpson's book *Touching the Void*, having rescued himself from a crevasse and with a badly broken leg, Joe had to crawl down the glacier and across a boulder field to get back to base camp. It was a massive undertaking for a person with a broken leg, no food, and badly dehydrated but he made it by setting small goals of reaching the next boulder in a certain time. Taking it one boulder at a time, he took three days to cover the distance, but he did it.

Similarly, I've run several half marathons now and although for me it seems like a massive distance, when I start out I don't think about the 13 miles ahead of me. I just think about making it to the first mile marker, and then the next one, and so on.

The bigger picture can be daunting, but focusing on smaller goals helps you make the final distance.

If you don't need to complete the small tasks in a particular order, then do the most difficult one first. Get it out of the way and then you can get on with the rest of the day knowing that the worst is behind you.

## Being firm with yourself

Sometimes the easiest way to manage your time and get something done is to just do it! Putting something off like a phone call or an email? Instead of saying to yourself, yet again, 'I'll do it in a minute' or 'I'll do it later' – do it now! Get the task out of the way and then you can move on and stop worrying.

I find this technique works really well if I've been putting something off for a while, usually something that's not immediately important. I don't even think about whether I want to do the job, I just do it.

## Letting go of problem tasks

If you hate cleaning, filing, admin, doing your books, mowing the lawn, you're probably going to put these tasks off until you absolutely *have* to do them. So instead of letting these jobs hang about, festering and niggling at you, get someone else to do them and spend your time on more productive things. Chapter 11 gives you the low-down on how to delegate.

If a task is worth doing, do it. If it's not, then just let it go and stop spending your time worrying about it.

## Using a carrot-and-stick approach

Give yourself a reward to balance the effort you're putting into achieving your goals – especially for the tasks you have a habit of putting off.

If you have a list of several tasks to do, the chances are you do the more interesting or fun ones first and leave the others. Do it the other way around. Reward yourself with the fun tasks *after* you've done some of the others.

# Having a focus day

Having a focus day is a great way to break your procrastination and get things done. Set aside a whole day or a few hours when you can team up with one or more friends or work colleagues.

Agree a start and end time and make a list of all the tasks you'd like to achieve within that time frame. You may want to clear a specific work project, declutter a room, clean the house, or catch up on filing. For example, you may want to:

✔ Catch up on emails (30 minutes).

✔ Make phone calls (45 minutes).

✔ Clear desk (1 hour).

✔ Organise the office (2 hours).

✔ Complete an outstanding report (2 hours).

✔ Tidy the bathroom and kitchen (30 minutes each).

✔ Update client files (30 minutes).

If you're not physically working together, set up a group call via a free conference call service such as www.freeconference.com or on Skype.

Check in with each other every hour. Let each other know what you're going to do in the next hour and then update everyone on what you've achieved when you next check-in. (Don't spend too much time on the call though, because you need the hour to complete your tasks!)

At the end of the day, give yourself a huge pat on the back, prepare a treat for yourself for all your effort, put your feet up and relax for a well earned rest!

I run regular Focus Days throughout the year – check my website at www.clareevans.co.uk for details.

As you plan your day, include a reward – this can be anything from taking a break for a coffee, meeting a friend for lunch, buying a CD you've been wanting, or going out for the evening, depending on the size of the task and effort involved. For a long-term project, book a treat – such as a trip to the theatre or a concert – in advance, so you can work towards it. Check out Chapter 10 for more on rewards.

# Getting Off the Fence and Making Decisions

Procrastination has a close cousin: indecisiveness. People sometimes find great excuses for procrastinating when they have a decision to make, because they're worried about making the wrong decision.

A little procrastination can be useful in decision-making. Making the right decision can take time. You want space to mull over the options, or you want to wait until you're in the right frame of mind. Sometimes, when you delay a decision the correct path becomes clear to you (or perhaps the need for the decision disappears).

But at times you become paralysed, unable to commit to a decision when you really need to. You ponder and deliberate, dissect and evaluate. You waste precious time going round in circles and getting nowhere fast. Sound familiar? Read on to discover how to break out of indecision.

## Brainstorming your options

A good starting point when you're struggling with a decision is to put things down on paper instead of mulling them over in your head. Grab a sheet of paper and a pen, and jot down the basics:

- ✔ What either/or decision must you make?
- ✔ What factors affect your decision?
- ✔ What are the anticipated outcomes for each possible choice?
- ✔ What can you gain from each option, and what might you lose?
- ✔ Is there a time limit to when you need to make the decision? (If there's no deadline, set one for yourself.)
- ✔ What will happen if you don't make a decision?

> ✔ What are your priorities?
>
> ✔ Does making this decision get you closer to your goals?

You need to make an informed decision, so make sure that you have all the facts and figures you need.

Jot down any ideas that come to mind. Sometimes the most obvious option isn't the best one. Write down *all* your different options, no matter how ridiculous they may seem.

## Weighing up the pros and cons

Sometimes, the best way to make a decision is to write down the pros and cons for each option. List the important criteria for making this decision. Don't get into too much detail – just make a note of the important, absolute must-haves.

Sometimes, your decision may be as simple as picking the option with the most pros (or the least cons). But often, pros and cons have different levels of importance, or you find it hard to decide. In this situation, use a rating system.

Make a list of all the factors in your decision. Then take each factor in turn and rate its importance for each of the options on a scale of 1 (low) to 5 (high). Add up your scores against each option. Sometimes it's easier to be objective if you put a number against things. If you've been honest, rating your options gives you a clearer idea of which option rates more highly and is the right choice.

For example, Ally is trying to decide whether to take a new job, or stay in his current position. Table 2-2 shows how he rates the factors for each choice he can make.

| Table 2-2 | Ally's Ratings Breakdown | |
| --- | --- | --- |
| *Factors* | *Taking New Job* | *Sticking with Current Job* |
| Location | 4 | 5 |
| Money | 5 | 3 |

*(continued)*

**Table 2-2 *(continued)***

| Factors | Taking New Job | Sticking with Current Job |
|---|---|---|
| Benefits | 4 | 4 |
| Working hours | 4 | 5 |
| Travel time | 5 | 4 |
| Career prospects | 5 | 2 |
| Job skill development | 5 | 2 |
| Job security | 3 | 5 |
| People | 4 | 4 |
| **Total** | 39 | 34 |

As you can see, taking the job slightly outweighs staying put for Ally. However, because the totals for each option are close, Ally may still find it hard to choose between the two options. In this case, he needs to check what his gut instinct is saying (see the later section 'Trusting your intuition').

When making any big decision, consider the risks involved. You may decide to go for a lower risk option rather than a potentially better decision but with a higher risk. For example, Ally may decide to stay in his current position because his job is more secure, there's a baby on the way, and bills to pay.

## Stepping back and seeing the full picture

Don't look at your options in isolation – consider how your decision can affect the rest of your life, and the impact it may have on your friends, family, work, and social life – your bigger picture.

Chapter 1 helps you think about setting goals. When making any decision, you need to keep in mind how the choice affects your longer-term goals and the impact it has on the time available to complete them. Conflicting decisions can arise when short-term rewards come up against long-term benefits. For example:

✔ 'I want to lose weight – I want to eat that slice of choco-late cake.'

✔ 'I want save up for a holiday – I want to buy that suit.'

✔ 'I want to leave work early – I have a report to get finished.'

✔ 'I want to spend more time with my family – my job is very demanding.'

Think about what matters more to you in this situation. Usually, achieving the long-term goal outweighs the short-term gain.

You also need to put your decision in perspective against the rest of your life. Just how important is this choice? How big is the impact? Try rating importance on a scale of one to ten:

✔ A level 1 decision is choosing a sandwich. Which sand-wich you choose doesn't really matter, because you'll feel less hungry, whatever you eat.

✔ A level 10 decision is choosing whether to jump out of the path of an oncoming car. The consequences of this deci-sion are life and death. (Not many decisions are level 10s!)

Got a level 1 or 2 decision on your hands? Do you really need to waste hours mulling over a decision that isn't worth the time and effort? Spending all morning deciding between a cup of tea and a cup of coffee isn't an effective use of your time. Okay, that's an extreme example, but you get the point.

## Getting a different perspective

Sometimes you can get too bogged down in the detail or the whole decision-making process. Here are some ideas for giving you a different outlook, allowing you to think about your problem differently and come to a decision:

✔ **Get away:** How often have you gone away on holiday only to make some important and potentially life-changing decisions? A change of scenery can work wonders. Go for a walk, or go away for a weekend. When you get a chance to switch off from the daily routine, you often see things more clearly.

✔ **Get some advice:** Ask a friend or colleague for her input and perspective. You can even ask someone to decide for you, but this isn't ideal – you need to own your decisions.

✔ **Put yourself in someone else's shoes:** Take yourself out of the situation – if someone else was making the decision what would they do?

✔ **Relax:** Stop thinking about the decision for a while. Check out Chapter 15 for time out ideas.

✔ **Sleep on it:** Your subconscious takes a look at the options as you rest, and the morning often brings new-found clarity.

Try not to make important decisions when you're tired or not functioning at your best.

## *Trusting your intuition*

Your intuition is a powerful and much underrated tool. Make every effort to use it. Your gut instinct tells you if and when you make the right or wrong decision.

---

# Heads or tails?

This is a good one for getting in touch with your intuition. If you really can't decide and you have two choices, toss a coin. When the coin lands, pay attention to your reaction when you see which side is showing. Your gut instinct tells you if the coin made the right choice for you.

For example, say heads represents moving house and tails represents staying put. When the coin lands, the Queen's face is looking up at you. How do you feel? If your gut reaction is happiness or relief, then you know that you should move house. But if you feel disappointed or unhappy at the result of the coin toss, and find yourself wishing it had been tails, you know that you don't want to move.

---

If you have all the facts and information in front of you, your subconscious can evaluate the data and come up with a gut reaction based on previous experience. It assimilates information much faster than your brain can think things through rationally and logically.

How has your intuition served you in the past? Do you normally make the right decision when you go with your gut reaction? Listen to it more and use it as a guide.

 If you're in touch with your gut instinct, you can take the plunge and make decisions quickly. If you're stuck and wasting time going back and forth, trying to decide, just make a decision. Doing something is often better than doing nothing. And occasionally you won't know if it's the right decision or not until you've made it.

## *Dealing with the aftermath of a decision*

Once you've made a decision, take action. No more wavering.

If you feel that you've made a wrong decision, don't panic. Instead, think about what knowledge you can take from the process. Ask yourself:

- ✔ Why was this choice wrong for me?
- ✔ Could I have done something different in the original decision-making process?
- ✔ Did I make the best decision possible, based on the facts and information available at the time?
- ✔ What do I want to do differently in the future?

On the whole you won't make many wrong decisions, especially if you weigh up the options carefully (see the earlier sections 'Brainstorming your options' and 'Weighing up the pros and cons') and listen to your instincts (see 'Trusting your intuition'). Take responsibility for your decisions once you've made them, and see them as part of your development process.

We all make a bad decision sometimes – the important thing is how you choose to move on from your 'mistake'. Don't forget that one of the definitions of a successful person is someone who has fallen down six times and got up seven.

# Part II
# Getting Your Time in Order

"He says he prefers makng notes as he finds it saves him time."

## *In this part . . .*

**Y**ou find out the importance of planning to increase your productivity and how you can use your diary to organise all the things you need to do each day. To-do lists can be more of a burden than a blessing, so find out how to make them work more effectively. This part also includes one of the more important skills you need to hone when it comes to managing your time – how to set boundaries and say *no* more often.

# Chapter 3

# Putting Everything in Its Place

••••••••••••••••••••••••••••••••••••••••••••••••

### In This Chapter

▶ Using diaries, planners, organisers, and computer tools

▶ Handling contact information

▶ Keeping tabs on important items and info

••••••••••••••••••••••••••••••••••••••••••••••••

*C*reating systems that help you better organise your work and time makes life a lot easier. 'Yikes,' I hear you right-brained, creative types say. 'Systems; we don't 'do' systems.' Fear not. In this chapter, I give you a variety of ideas and suggestions. Pick a solution that appeals, and adapt it to fit the way that you like to work.

Also in this chapter I touch on the importance of putting things in logical places – whether it's adding an appointment to your diary or a contact to your address book, or leaving your car keys somewhere more sensible than 'on the side'. Having a place for everything and putting everything in its place saves you time, makes life easier, and reduces frustration.

## Using Tools to Manage Your Time

Planning and organising your time doesn't need to be hard work. Use the following handy tools – in combination or alone – to improve your time management.

# Keeping a diary (just one, mind)

Most people have a diary, either paper-based or on their computer, perhaps even two – one for business, one for personal use. Some people have even more – one at work, one at home, and a personal one – but quite a few people don't have any system at all, keeping it all in their head or relying on other people.

Having a diary makes it a lot easier to keep track of things. But in order to organise your time most effectively, keep just *one* diary and write in it *all* your personal and business appointments. That way, you always have all important dates and events available when you're planning your time and booking appointments. You don't end up missing important events or having to juggle or cancel activities at the last minute because you've booked an important meeting for the same afternoon as your children's sports day.

You can use diaries for all sorts of appointments, not just meetings. Make an appointment with yourself when you need to set aside time for specific tasks.

How do you pick the right diary? If you choose paper-based, it doesn't matter if it's a page-a-day, or a week-at-a-view, as long as your diary is big enough and has enough space to write down everything you need to schedule in during your day. If you work on an hour-by-hour basis with several clients and customers you may need a page-a-day diary with space for notes. If you only attend a few meetings during the week, a week-at-a-view or two-days-to-a-page may be enough. An A5 diary is ideal and easier to carry around in a briefcase or handbag but decide what size you need based on how you're going to use it. Electronic diaries are only useful when you're working on your computer and unless you print them out or synchronise them with a hand-held device, they're not very portable.

Use colour, symbols, and images to make your daily calendar more fun and visual and to distinguish between different types of appointments, such as:

- Admin
- Holiday

> ✔ Meetings
>
> ✔ Personal/fun time
>
> ✔ Planning time
>
> ✔ Training/courses

Review your diary every day so you know not only what's coming up in the day but what's happening the following day and for the rest of the week. Review your monthly planner every week and your yearly planner at least once a month.

## Seeing the big picture on a wall planner

As well as having a daily diary, having a planner pinned up on the wall is often useful. You can use a monthly calendar, or a large year planner that provides you with a big picture view of the whole year at a glance and also lets other people around you know what's happening or where you are.

In the office, a team may have one planner to track holidays, training, and out-of-office days. If you all use the same one, you know who's doing what, when and can avoid conflicts – particularly with holidays. If everyone uses the wall planner, you can colour code who's who. Software sharing applications often enable teams to share their diaries electronically, so you can check who's where. However, having a wall planner pinned up in the office is quicker and easier to check.

At home you can have a large month or year planner for all the family to use – tracking holidays, important school days, family birthdays, social events, work commitments, and doctors' or dentist appointments.

Having one diary for both business and personal use doesn't mean that you can't use it in conjunction with a larger scale planner. Just get into the habit of updating it once a week. Make a note every Monday, Friday, or over the weekend to add any new 'big picture' appointments, meetings, or deadlines to your wall planner.

## Getting in sync

Make sure that all your various systems – such as your phone and PDA – are in sync with one another. Technology has made synchronisation easy to do as software that comes with the device automatically updates changes from the hand-held device to your computer system and vice versa via a cable or docking station.

You can update appointments and contact details and they automatically update both systems when you sync up, saving the time of manual updates.

To keep your records up to date and protected, synchronise regularly. You'll thank me for this advice when (not if) your PDA's battery goes flat. You can quickly update it from your computer. Just think how much time you'd spend if you had to re-key the information again.

## *Keeping it together with a personal organiser*

Whether electronic or paper-based, personal organisers expand the function of a basic diary and can make life easier by allowing you to put all your essential information in one place. You don't have to carry around a diary, address book, *and* your action list separately.

Paper-based personal organisers, like Filofax and Franklin Organisers, come in all shapes and sizes. You can have page-a-day, or week-at-a-view, and there's usually space to jot down appointments, lists, and notes. Other features may include fold-out year planners, birthday planners, expense lists, and to-do lists. Find a size and format that suits the way you work and how you're going to use it.

Electronic personal organisers (also known as Personal Digital Assistants, or PDAs) such as the Palm Pilot, iPAQ, and even some models of mobile phones, fit easily into a pocket. Most PDAs also have the added functionality of being able to plug in to your computer and automatically synchronise with your

computer system's diary and contacts (see the si.
'Getting in sync'). Automatic synchronisation saves ,
having to manually re-type any updates. Skip to Chaptɩ
more details on these useful gadgets.

## Logging on to computer-based tools

Most computers come with an electronic calendaring system
that provides a diary and address book facility. Microsoft
Outlook is one of the most popular for Windows-based
machines but others are available – some of which link in with
your email system and automatically update your email contacts, and you can schedule appointments via email.

> ✔ **Outlook** provides a calendar, address book, task list, and
> email system all in one application. You can change the
> layout to suit the way you work, schedule in reminders,
> and book in appointments.
>
> Online calendaring tools are also available, usually with
> your web-based email system that synchronises with
> your computer or hand-held device, enabling you to
> access your calendar when you're not at your desk. If you
> want, you can share your calendar across the web, choos-
> ing which events you share and who has access to them.
>
> ✔ **Plaxo**, an online address book, is a convenient and time-
> saving way to keep up-to-date and manage and backup
> your contact system online. Plaxo automatically keeps
> you updated if your friends' and colleagues' details
> change. You choose what information you share and who
> sees it and you can have different access for personal
> and business contacts. Plaxo includes a calendar (which
> automatically updates from Outlook). You can find out
> more at www.plaxo.com.

## Tackling Forgetfulness with Systematic Reminders

How good are you at remembering to do things? Do you forget
to make a phone call you agreed to? Do you forget things that

need to be done on a certain day or at a particular time? Unless you have a photographic memory, carrying around a lot of information in your head is a recipe for disaster. Instead, choose a simple system that remembers the important stuff for you. You save time by entering information just once and then have it remind you automatically each week, month, or year.

## Setting automated reminders

If you use Microsoft Outlook or a similar electronic calendaring system (see the earlier section 'Logging on to computer-based tools'), why not use the reminder's function to nudge your memory about things you need to do?

To set a reminder, first you need to create an appointment in the system. Then, you can tell the system to send you reminders at specific times before the appointment. You can tell the system to pop up an alert, so you won't miss the reminder.

You can set the system to remind you to:

- Book your car for its annual MOT/service.
- Chase someone for a piece of work.
- Follow-up on a phone call.
- Pay a bill each month.
- Post a birthday card.
- Return your library books.
- Update your accounts.

Reminders come in handy especially for future tasks that seem a long way off, which you're likely to forget about. For example, if you need to follow up with your clients or customers every few months or once a year, set up a reminder and then you can relax, knowing you'll follow up at the right time.

Here are some general tips on setting reminders:

- Set an appointment on the system for early morning. This ensures that it pops up first thing, ready for when you start work.

> ✓ If you need a regular reminder for something – for example, every Friday you need to backup the data on your computer or update your accounts – create a recurring appointment.

> ✓ If you write a regular newsletter, article or report, set a reminder a week before you need to write it, then schedule the time in your diary to do it. Have a second reminder the day before it needs to go out. It's a great way to manage your schedule, which in turn manages your time.

 Use your paper diary for reminders in the same way. Just add an entry one or two days or a week in advance. Use a symbol or colour to highlight the entry as a reminder rather than an appointment.

## Checking in on files

Another way of remembering to do things on a certain day is to use a day file. Buy one of those expanding files with a pocket for each day. If you have a piece of work or a phone call that needs to be made on a particular day, write it on a piece of paper and pop it into the appropriate pocket. Check your day file first thing every morning and get out the relevant reminders and actions for that day.

Similarly, have another expanding file or a folder for each month. As the paperwork comes in, or if you have something that needs to be done in a particular month, place it in the file. For example, you may use your monthly folder for:

✓ Your Tax Return in September or January.

✓ Ideas for presents on a Christmas shopping list.

✓ Checklist for your holiday.

✓ Annual insurance reminder.

Each month, look ahead to see what you need to do the following month.

BRIGHT IDEA

## Oops – I forgot your birthday!

How good are you at remembering birthdays and anniversaries? Is it a bit hit and miss? Do you remember on the day or, even worse, the following day?

Here are some tips to help you avoid that toe-curling 'sorry, I forgot' confession:

✔ Add birthdays to your diary, and check ahead once in a while to see what's coming up.

✔ Buy a specific birthday book. You can keep all the important dates in one place, and transfer them from one year to the next.

✔ Use a contact system like Outlook and Plaxo. You can enter the date of birth, or at least the birthday, alongside your contact information. It's then automati-

cally added to the calendar. As long as you check your calendar on a regular basis you'll be reminded in advance of upcoming birthdays.

✔ Sign up to an electronic greetings card provider. They remind you of upcoming birthdays and you can send an electronic greetings card too.

✔ If you *really* want to be organised and save time, buy all your birthday cards at the beginning of the year and put them in a monthly folder (one of those expanding files does the job). Print off a birthday list and put it at the front. It's easy to see whose birthday is coming up each month.

# *Managing Your Contact Information*

You need to keep a wealth of information on people, such as their name, phone numbers – home, office, mobile – email address, mailing address, and fax number. And details such as addresses and mobile numbers change regularly.

Don't squander time rooting about for numbers scribbled on scraps of paper, or fighting through the cobwebs in your mind for someone's surname – set up an organised contact system.

You can choose to keep your contact information in an address book, on index cards or on an electronic contact system. Either option is fine – just make sure that you stick with one and keep it up to date.

## Entering contact details

Enter new or updated contact information in your address book or computer system as soon as possible, or set aside time once a week when you update all the new contact information you've collected during the week.

Carry two business card holders in your pocket or bag. Use one for your own cards and one for people you've met. Make a note on the back of their card about where you met and any relevant information. Store cards in a small box or envelope until they're updated, and then store them in a business card box file.

## Categorising your contacts

Your list of contacts isn't just useful to you but may be useful to someone else too. How often do people ask you, 'Do you know someone who . . .?' If someone needs an accountant, electrician or plumber, for example, you can use your contact information to see if you know anyone who can.

Group your contacts into different categories for personal, business, or specific projects. They'll be easier to find. If you're using a paper-based system, get out the coloured pens.

## Using notes

Many address books also include space for notes. Use this space for additional information about your contacts. You may jot down details such as:

- ✔ Where and when you first met them.
- ✔ Notes about their business.
- ✔ When you last contacted them.
- ✔ Personal info, such as mutual friends and shared interests.

On a computer system, these fields may be searchable, which makes it quicker to find the relevant contact when you need it – such as all the people you met at a particular meeting last year.

## Creating distribution lists

You're probably familiar with distribution lists. You've no doubt found yourself on a few (whether you wanted to be or not).

Adding your contacts to different distribution lists is useful and saves time if you need to contact several people at once. For example:

- ✔ You meet a group of people at a meeting and you want to follow up with them all on a regular basis.

- ✔ You want to contact all the people in your immediate area about an up-coming event.

- ✔ You need to send a relevant piece of information to people who work for a particular company or industry.

- ✔ You're working with several people on a project and you need to send them regular updates.

You can use a distribution list over and over again, so you don't waste time searching through and selecting individual names each time. Use as many as you need: they can be permanent groups that you use all the time or temporary ones for a specific project or event.

When you go on holiday, print off a sheet of address labels to take with you. You save time handwriting all those addresses on your postcards – time you can spend sunning yourself or browsing cheesy souvenir shops.

# Now, 1 Know that 1 Put It Somewhere . . .

You know how it is, you're rushing out to work and you can't find your keys. You know that you put them down somewhere when you came in last night. You write down an important number and then lose it amongst all your various post-it notes you've got stuck everywhere. You put that important piece of paper to one side for later and now you can't find it.

Sound familiar? Create a place for all these things to go and you're less likely to lose them or forget where you put them in the first place.

Having a place for everything and putting everything in its place saves you time, makes life easier, and reduces frustration.

## Creating a home for the essentials

Have a drop-off point by the door to your home. A small tray or bowl works well. As soon as you come in at the end of the day, dump your keys, mobile phone, and wallet into it. That way you know exactly where they are when you leave for work the next morning or go out later, and you won't waste time searching round for those things.

Do the same in the office – have a drawer, shelf, or bowl on your desk that these things can go into. Have a lockable drawer or cabinet for your valuables.

## Keeping important information handy

Avoid ending up with lots of scraps of paper and lists all over the place. Instead, carry a notebook with you everywhere you go. Use it to jot down notes, ideas, thoughts, actions, and your action lists (see Chapter 4) as well as contact details for people you meet. You then know where that important piece of information is and as part of your daily planning (and when you have a few spare minutes) you can go through and review what you've written and update your contacts list or diary.

If something doesn't fit into any obvious 'place', designate a bits and bobs drawer, file, or folder where it can find a temporary home until you decide what to do with it. Then, if you're searching around for something, you can check your bits and bobs first and likely find what you need. Once in a while, have a clear out – if you haven't looked at or used something in months, then you can probably safely bin it.

As for paperwork, read Chapter 7 to sort out specific places for that.

# Chapter 4

# Organising Your Time and Your Tasks

*I*n this chapter I show you ways to structure and organise your time in the most effective way so that you get focused but also remain flexible. If you can't do everything, you need to know how to identify your most important tasks and what needs to be done first.

In this chapter you discover how to tackle those never-ending to-do lists and create something that's more realistic, productive, and actually works.

## Structuring Your Time

Successful time management isn't rocket science; it goes hand in hand with effectively organising your time. The following sections help you think about the best ways to plan and spend your time.

### Creating blocks of time

Divide your day into blocks of time. Not only does doing this make it easier to plan and organise your day in advance, you also make better use of your time. Focusing on one task at a time is much more efficient than switching from one task to another as things pop into your head.

If you have regular tasks that you do every week, block out the same time each week. For example, if you do your accounts on a weekly basis, block out an hour or so on a Friday morning or Monday afternoon, or book time out a couple of days before the end of the month.

### Setting aside communication time

Create blocks of time in which you handle communications – emails and outgoing phone calls. Don't fall into the trap of tackling emails and calls in dribs and drabs, otherwise you get sucked into spending longer than you intended. Set aside designated time, lay down a time limit, and stick to it.

Although it's not usually practical to set aside blocks of time for incoming calls, you can minimise the disruption of the constant brrrring. Switch on your answerphone or turn off your mobile for the time when you need to focus, then return calls later (during your designated time for making outgoing calls).

Chapter 8 gives you much more detail on how to deal with your emails quickly and easily, and Chapter 9 has the low-down on managing your phone calls effectively.

### Blocking out focused time

Some jobs, such as writing a report or proofreading a newsletter, require your complete concentration. To ensure that you can give the task the attention it requires, block out time in your diary.

If you just leave doing a task to when you feel like it, you find other things take priority. But if you've already scheduled in the time for the task, there's less reason to put it off or be interrupted by other work coming in. Your time is already committed.

If you need some quiet, creative time, go somewhere different, away from the distractions of your normal workspace. For example, getting up early and working from home for a couple of hours enables you to get more done away from the distractions of the office.

### Factoring in circumstances

Unless you're clairvoyant, you can't plan for every eventuality. For example:

- ✔ Your boss turns up and asks you to do an urgent piece of work by the end of the day. (Make sure that you read Chapter 5 on setting boundaries before you happily agree to drop everything to slot in this task.)

- ✔ You come up against a problem and it takes time to fix. For example, your computer crashes just at the critical moment and you lose everything you've been working on. You have to wait a day or so for the repair, or you have to rely on your backups. (You do back up, don't you? If not, take a look at Chapter 7 quick smart!)

- ✔ A report you're writing needs a vital piece of information and you can't get hold of the person who can provide it because he or she is away on holiday until next week.

- ✔ You get a call reminding you about a piece of work you'd forgotten about and you need to get it done now.

- ✔ You underestimate how long a task takes.

When scheduling, bear in mind that the best-laid plans often don't go quite as expected. Build a bit of contingency into your time planning. You'll be glad of that extra time if a task takes longer than you anticipated, and your day won't be thrown into total disarray when something crops up. Plus, if you don't need the extra leeway you build into your day, you'll have a bit of slack time (check out Chapter 17 for ideas on how to make good use of this spare time).

In addition, bear the following in mind when blocking out time in your diary:

- ✔ When you book a meeting in your diary, the time involved isn't just about the meeting itself. You may have preparation work to do, travel time, and after the meeting, follow-up and minutes or a report to produce. Block out time for both pre- and post-meeting work as well as the event itself.

✔ Be aware of the energy requirements of different days (see the following section 'Working with your natural tendencies'). If you've had an intense day of meetings, book in some time for admin work or for catching up. Training courses and workshops can be mentally and physically demanding – whether you're the one giving them or participating.

✔ When you get back from holiday, set aside at least the first half-day for dealing with your emails and paperwork, otherwise you fall straight back into work mode and never catch up. Try not to book up a heavy day of meetings for your first day back, so that you have time to catch up or check in with your staff or colleagues.

Your aim is not to have a full diary. You can guarantee that if you've allocated all your time, your boss comes along with a high priority task and you then need to drop everything and re-jig your plans to fit the new work in. You need space between your blocks of time, not only for unexpected tasks but for breaks too. Don't try to cram too much in on one day.

## Working with your natural tendencies

As I mention in Chapter 1, we all like to work in different ways. When planning your time, work to your strengths and create a structure that best fits your natural tendencies.

Know when your most productive time of day is and when you prefer doing certain types of tasks and plan around those times:

✔ **Early bird:** Some people work best first thing in the morning, which can be a good time for creativity. If you find you're more efficient and productive in the morning, use the morning to do tasks that require you to be at your best or need your concentration. Don't set aside time to work on a complex report or something that requires your concentration in the afternoon when you're more likely to hit the post-lunch slump, or in the evening when you're tired.

Try getting up an hour or so earlier to make the best use of your productive time of day. But don't burn the candle at both ends and go to bed late as well!

✔ **Night owl:** Some people get steadily more alert and effective as the day goes on. Perhaps you struggle to get going in the morning and feel as if you're just ticking over, but are turbo-charged after lunch and into the evening. You may find you focus best late at night, when it's quiet. If this is you, plan your day around your tendencies. Don't try getting up at 6 a.m. to write a report if you know you can do it better and quicker at 2 p.m.

Also think about how the week pans out for you. Certain days of the week may make better sense when scheduling in particular tasks. For example, you may hit the ground running on a Monday morning but be ready to go home by Thursday. Alternatively, you may find you have a peak of activity on a Friday when you're keen to clear things out at the end of the week and go home with a clean slate.

Be aware of your energy levels, both throughout the day and at different times of the week, month or year – wintertime and less daylight can slow people down. When you're tired or under the weather, you won't be able to get as much done. Keep this fact in mind and give yourself permission to do less at these times. Focus on the 80/20 – do the really important things that add the most value when time is short or when your energy isn't up to it (refer to Chapter 1).

Try not to fight your natural tendency to schedule work when you feel at your best. If you're tied to traditional office hours then when you start and finish work may not be entirely your decision. But many employers now offer more flexible working patterns, and you can choose how you spend your time before and after work. Of course, if you work for yourself you have more flexibility around when you work – see Chapter 12 for ideas on how to structure your day.

## Doing varied tasks, little and often

Your mind can easily become bored if you spend too long on a particular task. So don't plan to sit down for hours on end focusing on just one task in a long, intense session. Break a task down into small bites and work through little and often (refer to Chapter 2 for more on breaking down tasks).

The longer you spend doing one thing, the more ineffective you actually become. You're more efficient and productive when you do short bursts of activity:

- ✔ You won't get so distracted if you know you've only got a limited amount of time on which to work on a task.

- ✔ Time out during a task refreshes you. Your mind has a chance to process things and you can come up with new thoughts and solutions, particularly if you have a difficult problem to deal with or a mental block.

- ✔ Having a time limit – such as 10, 20, or 30 minutes – can increase the rate at which you work, so you actually get more done.

- ✔ Working on a difficult or odious task for just a short period of time doesn't seem as bad as having to do it all in one go!

And while you're blocking out short amounts of time for tasks, you can also introduce a bit of variety to spice up your day. Injecting a bit of variety into your everyday work helps you keep interested, energetic, and motivated.

Consider the following ideas:

- ✔ Mix high-energy or intense tasks with something less demanding. Work hard, and then sit back a bit. Spread out your energy.

- ✔ Switch from a task that requires you to be analytical to one that requires you to work more creatively. Think about engaging the left and right sides of your brain as you work. You'll find you're able to focus better.

- ✔ Can you do the same thing in a different location? Working from home or working at a different office from time to time can add variety to your working environment, keeping your mind stimulated.

## Scheduling in 'me time'

Spending all day sitting at your desk, hunched over your computer keyboard, or with the phone attached to your head, leaves you tired, both physically and mentally.

Include breaks in the structure of your day:

- ✔ Do some stretches (Chapter 17 has some great tension-relieving desk stretches).

- ✔ Step away from your desk and walk around the office, or even better, get outside for some freshair.

- ✔ Grab a healthy snack or a drink of water.

- ✔ Take some quiet time and just relax.

Building 'me time' into your day is just as important as fitting in the million and one jobs you have to do. Take a look at Chapter 15 for lots of ideas on how to look after yourself.

# Organising Your Tasks

The following sections have one key, unifying theme – lists. Forget relying on your memory to tell you everything you need to do, or working amid piles of scribbled to-do lists – in the following sections, I show you how using simple lists helps you to manage your workload effectively.

## Binning to-do lists

If you're like most people, you have a to-do list. Your list likely consists of an A4 sheet of paper (or several) or perhaps a document on your computer. You continually add tasks to the list and occasionally cross things off.

Actually I don't like using to-do lists and I suspect others don't either. Such lists can be a bit of a double-edged sword. Although they're a useful tool when used correctly – and they create structure in a busy day – the items on the list have a tendency to be things you *want* to do and not things that actually get done.

## Tips for effective studying

Your mind is alert and active for only a short period of time before concentration drops off. So cramming days before an exam may be a favourite solution for some, but it isn't a very effective way of revising. Instead, follow these tips when you need to remember information:

✔ For optimal concentration and information retention, divide your time into blocks of an hour. In each hour, work for 50 minutes, and then take a 10-minute break.

✔ Review at regular intervals the material previously studied to move it from short-term to long-term memory. The following day spend a few minutes reviewing all the material from the previous day. Each week spend a few minutes reviewing all the material revised in the previous week. Each month review the material revised in the previous month.

✔ Study little and often. Better to study for an hour a day for three weeks, than for two days solid.

Your to-do list then becomes a source of frustration and stress. You constantly add tasks, and end up demoralised and overwhelmed as the list grows longer and longer and you never seem to get to the end of it.

My advice? Ditch the to-do list, and instead, use action lists (see the following sections). An *action list* comprises tasks you're going to action rather an endless list of jobs that you'd get round to . . . if only you had the time.

## Deciding what belongs on your action list

In Chapter 1, I help you identify your overall goals – both personal and business. When putting together an action list, you need to keep a close eye on how tasks fit in with your goals. By focusing on your goals you can identify the important tasks and ignore the trivial tasks that are likely to lead you off in the wrong direction or distract you from your main purpose.

Ask yourself what you want to achieve in the next week or the next month. Then take each task in turn, and ask how it fits with your goals for the short and long term.

 Your lists need to be manageable. One thing is certain – you're never going to be able to do everything on your list if you just keep adding to it. There really aren't enough hours in the day. Don't give yourself a hard time and set unrealistic expectations about what you're capable of doing in the time available.

 Get into the habit of reviewing and updating your lists regularly. Otherwise they end up becoming useless and more of an effort than an effective tool if they're forgotten or ignored.

## Prioritising your tasks

It's rarely possible to get everything done that you'd like to, so you have to make choices about what you need to work on. When you have a limited amount of time available you make a choice about what to work on immediately and what to leave until later – you *prioritise* your tasks.

You may choose to reorganise your filing system because it'll make finding things easier and you'll have a great sense of satisfaction when it's done. However, if you've chosen to do this instead of doing the report that your boss needs by the end of the day, you need to rethink your priorities.

Prioritising your tasks is essential. However many tasks you have on your list, you can establish a logical order in which they need to be done.

 Putting things off is a common reason for inefficiency (refer to Chapter 2). Well, prioritising blows procrastination out of the water. You have to tackle those important tasks first, rather than put them off in favour of easier, more enjoyable ones.

### Finding a method that suits you

Develop a method to organise your tasks in order of importance. Keep things simple with just three or four levels of priority.

You can split up tasks by using different systems such as:

- ✔ Must do, need to do, can do.
- ✔ High, Medium, Low.
- ✔ 1, 2, 3.
- ✔ A, B, C.
- ✔ Red, Amber, Green.

Don't make *all* your tasks high priority. Unless you've only got three things on your list, you won't manage to do them all.

Recognise the difference between an urgent task and an important task that shouts very loudly. For example, say you have three reports to write. Report A is due in two days and you haven't started it yet – that's *urgent*. Report B is due in two weeks and is *important* to a client your company is working with. Report C is also due in two weeks, but a colleague keeps asking for updates and pushing you to get on with it. Stick to your guns and do Report A first because that's the most urgent task. B and C are equally important but as your colleague is chasing C, you may decide to work on that one next. Head to Chapter 5 for loads more on setting expectations and managing deadlines when prioritising tasks.

When trying to decide how crucial a task is, don't belittle the important things in your life like your partner, family, friends, and your health. Make sure that you're prioritising time for them too.

### Working down the hierarchy

After you prioritise your tasks, you can work through them in order:

1. Always try to do the highest priority tasks first. Don't leave them to the last minute – get them out of the way as soon as possible.

2. Make sure that once you've cleared the *urgent* tasks you start to spend more of your time working on the *important* tasks. If you make this switch then they won't become urgent in the first place.

3. Finally, when you've ticked off the urgent and important tasks, tackle the unimportant tasks. These are your lower priority tasks.

Generally, you work through tasks in this order. However, don't feel constrained by your prioritised list. Sometimes, in the course of your working day, you can pick and mix tasks. For example, you may check emails before making an important phone call because the person isn't yet in the office.

 The important thing to remember is that, at the end of the day, you must have completed *all* the high priority tasks you scheduled for that day. If you didn't, you need to ask yourself what stopped you:

- ✔ Did you prioritise the task correctly? If not, can you see where you went wrong and remedy it for the next time?

- ✔ Were you distracted or interrupted? Chapter 10 has plenty of advice for you.

- ✔ Did you simply put the task off? Had this task become high priority because you've left it to the last minute? Flick to Chapter 2 to tackle procrastination.

At the other end of the list, you may find that you're not getting through the lower priority tasks. Don't worry – these trivial tasks have a natural tendency to become even less important and can finally be crossed off the list all together. Let the natural course of time dictate what falls off the bottom of the list. Anything serious or urgent finds its way to the top of the list.

As you get better at prioritising you'll start to recognise certain tasks that you're just not going to have time for and they won't even make it onto the list.

## Setting up action lists

Avoid *listitis* – creating lists for the sake of it. You may feel as though you're being organised, but not if you don't actually do anything with the list. Rather than having different lists scattered all over the place, stick to just two lists: a Master List and a Daily Action List.

 Keeping your lists together in one place means that you can keep track of all your projects and actions. Keep your lists in a loose-leaf binder, pinned to your notice board, or in your diary, notebook, or organiser.

### Creating your Master List

Your Master List helps you to keep track of everything thing you want to get done. Put all the daily, weekly, and monthly actions on your Master List, as well as tasks and projects for the future that are part of your longer-term goals. Write things down on your Master List as a placeholder and a reminder for things that don't need doing immediately.

Table 4-1 shows an example of a Master List.

| Table 4-1 | Master Action List |
| --- | --- |
| **Task** | |
| Check emails (daily) | |
| Follow-up with all clients | |
| Update website | |
| Complete monthly newsletter | |
| Develop new project | |
| Update account | |
| Update tax information | |
| Complete audit | |
| Organise clients' files | |
| Sort through filing tray | |
| Read industry publications (weekly) | |
| Book up seminar | |
| Arrange training course for Q3 | |
| Carry out staff annual assessments | |

When your Master Lists gets too messy, or when most of the actions have been transferred, completed, or have become redundant, then rewrite it. It helps to keep the list fresh and easier to work with.

## Making a Daily Action List

The aim of a Daily Action List is that you're actually going to tick off every single item. For your action list to work, you need to be sensible when estimating how long each task will take (don't worry; this comes with experience).

Make time for a planning session each morning. Refer to your Master List and pick out the things you're going to get done that day. Write your tasks on your Daily Action List.

Don't make the mistake of listing out 20 things you need to do and then realising that they can take anything from 30 minutes to an hour to complete. Be realistic; you just don't have enough time in the day for everything. If you only have five things on your list and you cross them all off, that's far more effective, satisfying, and sensible than having a list of 20 items and only doing half of them. Action lists are all about getting away from the traditional, endless to-do list.

Table 4-2 shows a sample Daily Action List.

| Table 4-2 | Sample Daily Action List | |
|---|---|---|
| **Task** | **Priority** | **Time** |
| Check emails | 2 | 1 hour |
| Call John at xyz Company | 1 | 15 minutes |
| Order new supplies | 1 | 30 minutes |
| Finish Monthly Report | 2 | 2 hours |
| Prepare presentation | 2 | 1 hour |
| Write article | 3 | 2 hours |
| Collect dry cleaning | 2 | 30 minutes |

Note that the 'Priority' column helps you decide the order in which you need to do the jobs (see the earlier section 'Prioritising your tasks'). The 'Time' column gives you an idea of how long each task takes (see the earlier section 'Structuring your time').

Your list doesn't have to be just about work, after all, you can't always get your personal actions done outside of the 9–5 slot. Include everything you need to do in the day.

Keep referring to your Daily Action List throughout the day. Make sure that you complete the most important tasks by the end of each day. Don't get distracted if something new comes up during the day – jot it down on the Master List rather than adding it to your Daily Action List.

If you start to lose focus and find your mind wandering then it's probably time to take a break or to switch to something less taxing. See the earlier sections 'Doing varied tasks, little and often' and 'Scheduling in "me time"'.

## Creating checklists

In addition to crossing off the tasks on your Master and Daily Action Lists (see the preceding section), creating checklists for general and regular tasks helps you get organised, focused, and on track. Ticking off jobs gives you a sense of achievement and progression.

Create a template checklist on your computer. The advantage of using a computer-based template is that many of your tasks are the same from day to day or week to week. You can manage the checklist on your computer, or better still, print out the list and tick things off by hand. There's something quite satisfying about putting pen to paper.

Table 4-3 is a very simple checklist for a week. Simply tick off the tasks as you complete them.

| Table 4-3 | Sample Weekly Checklist | | | | |
|---|---|---|---|---|---|
| **No** | **Task** | **M** | **T** | **W** | **T** | **F** |
| 1 | Accounts | ✔ | | | | ✔ |
| 2 | Emails | ✔ | ✔ | ✔ | ✔ | ✔ |
| 3 | Filing | ✔ | ✔ | | | ✔ |

| No | Task | M | T | W | T | F |
|----|------|---|---|---|---|---|
| 4 | Weekly report | | | | ✔ | |
| 5 | Clear inbox | ✔ | ✔ | ✔ | ✔ | |

You can use similar checklists for your regular monthly tasks.

An erasable whiteboard can be a useful, larger, more visual reminder and planning tool. I have one in my office that I divide into different sections:

- ✔ Blogs
- ✔ Business
- ✔ Calls
- ✔ Emails
- ✔ Finance
- ✔ Personal

## Getting creative with your lists

Is there such a thing as stationery addiction? I love buying new stuff to organise my workspace. There's something satisfying about going out and buying new supplies, notebooks to write in, pens to write with, colourful gel pens, highlighters, marker pens, folders, post it pads. Okay – perhaps I have too much time on my hands or I need to get out more!

But getting in touch with your arty side not only makes list writing more fun, it can make the lists more effective. After all, the more fun, creative, and colourful you make your lists, the more likely you're going to want to work with them every day.

Here are some ideas:

- ✔ Use coloured pens to mark and prioritise your tasks. Tasks highlighted in red or green stand out and you're less likely to lose them. Use different colours for different areas of your life or for different projects.

- ✔ Use stickers and dots to distinguish between business and personal tasks.

- ✔ Use gold stars to highlight really important tasks or as a reward on your checklist.

You know how you work best, so find a style that suits you.

The headings stay the same from week to week, but the actions change. At the beginning of the week I write up all my weekly actions and then update it each day, crossing out or erasing the tasks I complete.

Create sections that are relevant to the way you work and under each section write your actions on a daily basis. If you don't have a whiteboard, a large sheet of paper on a notice board does the job.

Give yourself a reward at the end of the week if you manage to tick off all your tasks. These don't have be big rewards but the equivalent of a gold star – a little time for yourself at the end of the day, leaving work early. Skip over to Chapter 10 for more on motivating yourself with rewards.

# Chapter 5

# Setting Your Boundaries

- - - - - - - - - - - - - - - - - - - - - - - - - - - - - - - - - - - - - - - -

## *In This Chapter*

▶ Deciding where you draw the line

▶ Managing and setting expectations

▶ Letting go of the automatic urge to act

▶ Saying no confidently and effectively

- - - - - - - - - - - - - - - - - - - - - - - - - - - - - - - - - - - - - - - -

*G*ive an inch and they take a mile. At least, they will if you let them. The importance of creating boundaries around your time is that, like a physical boundary, doing so enables you to decide what you want to come in and what you want to keep out as you go about managing your time. By setting boundaries you define what you want and what you'll accept from your boss, your colleagues, your partner, your family, and your friends.

In this chapter I help you create clear boundaries for yourself and other people. By setting expectations you let people know what's acceptable and what's not, and you minimise stress and wasted time.

When it comes down to it, only one person decides how you're going to use your time – you. This chapter shows you how to exercise that power to choose, putting you firmly in control of your own time.

 Phone calls, emails, people popping by with inane questions – all these boundary-encroachers eat into your time. Flick to Chapters 8 and 9 to find out how to handle emails and phone calls efficiently, and to Chapter 10 for advice on how to deal with interruptions.

# Defining Your Boundaries

Setting clear boundaries both at work and in your personal life protects your time and space – resulting in an all-round happier lifestyle and a use of time that suits you.

After you define the limits that you're happy to accept, decide what you'll do if these boundaries are crossed. Having boundaries is no good if you don't defend them. And once in a while, check in on your boundaries. Although setting limits at the start might be easy, letting them slip is all too common. Make sure that your boundaries remain in place and no one's storming the ramparts.

## Drawing the line at work

What are your working hours? To a certain extent, your boss defines your work hours and makes them part of your work contract. But even when you have designated work hours, people trample over the boundaries.

People in the UK already work longer hours than their European counterparts and there's often an element of guilt if you're actually seen leaving work on time. Too often, you end up having to work late or go in early when you're up against a deadline or have too much work to do.

It doesn't take much to go from working an eight-hour day to working ten or more hours just by adding an hour at the beginning and end of each day – that's 25 per cent more. What impact does that have, not only on your hourly rate (see Chapter 1) but also your available 'free' time? Keep a check on the hours you work. Have they started to increase? Rein yourself back in and reset those time management boundaries.

Most of us are only paid to work a certain number of hours in a week. You can always find exceptions and you may be happy to get paid overtime or work a few extra hours every now and then, but it shouldn't become the norm or something that's expected. Don't let people take advantage of you and eat up your valuable time.

If you can't complete the work with the time available, take a look at the way you're working and what it is you're being asked to do. Organise your work to fit within your normal working hours. If you've been asked to do more than is achievable, push back. Explain to your boss your current workload and why you're not able to take on any more (you can find more on how to go about this in the later sections 'Setting Expectations' and 'Just Saying "No"'). Long hours and working weekends need to be the exception rather than the rule.

Working from home may give you greater flexibility around start and finish times, but it's just as important to make sure that you create structure around your day and have set times that you work. Setting a start and finish time for your work ensures that you avoid the temptation to work all hours. Chapter 12 has plenty of advice on setting boundaries when you work at home – from sticking to your working hours to letting friends and family know when to leave you alone so that you can get on.

If your family and friends complain that they never see you then perhaps that's a cue to cut down your working hours.

## Creating boundaries in your personal life

Your personal life is where boundaries tend to be non-existent or easily crumble. Giving in to demands from your partner, family, and friends is too easy. However, you need to think about what you want too, so don't always just give in to what everyone else wants. If you don't want every weekend taken up with social activities, set boundaries.

Be clear about what you will and won't do, and what your limits are. That way, you can avoid feeling stressed and pressurised when you're being pulled in several different directions.

Spend time with friends and family but also give yourself time and space. Ensure that you have one weekend a month when you're just at home and not out socialising or away visiting family and friends.

If you don't plan your time properly, then you can't complain when you find all your evenings and weekends are taken up with commitments. By putting *everything* down in your calendar, you can easily see how busy you are and when to stop.

# Setting Expectations

When things go wrong or you end up wasting time doing the wrong things, it's often because you haven't clearly defined what's expected. You haven't communicated what you want, or haven't understood what's expected of you.

When someone asks you to do something make sure that you know what it is that you're expected to do and how long it's likely to take, so that you know whether you have time for it. Equally, when you ask someone to do something make sure that you both understand what you're asking. No good asking for a Rolls Royce and getting a Mini.

When setting expectations for a task, cover each of the following:

✔ **What** specifically do you want me to do?

Get a clear picture of the nature and scope of the work and how long it's likely to take.

✔ **When** exactly do I need to complete this task?

A timeframe enables you to prioritise this piece of work more accurately. Do you need to complete the work now, this week, next month, or by the end of the year?

✔ **How** should I do the task?

Is there a particular way in which this task needs to be completed, which also lets you know how much time is involved? If you've an idea of how the job is going to be done, does it match what the other person wants?

✔ **Why** am I doing this?

Understand the reason for the what, when and how. For example, if the person giving you the work says, 'I'd like you to get this report completed by the end of next week ready for the management presentation on Monday,' you understand the urgency of the job.

These four questions help you set expectations when someone else is giving you something to do. You can also use them
when you're the person tasking someone else with a job.
Simply turn the questions around – what do I want you to do,
by when, how, and why? Flick to Chapter 11 for more tips on
effective delegation.

Clearly communicating expectations is important. Summarise
what's been requested to make sure that you've understood
clearly. Be informed rather than making assumptions. As one
of my bosses was fond of saying 'To assume makes an Ass of
U and an Ass of Me.' Well, I would never have called him an
ass and I don't think that he was the first to say it, but you can
see his point.

Check in every now and then when you're working on a task
for someone to make sure that nothing's changed. There's
nothing worse than completing a piece of work only to find
that it's no longer needed, or that they actually wanted you to
include xyz when you've done abc.

The one person who sets the highest expectation is often
yourself. You want everything to be perfect so you spend
hours dotting the i's and crossing the t's when actually it's not
necessary. Good time management involves simply doing the
job required. Just because you *can* do more, doesn't mean
you should. So if your boss asks you to make a simple table
showing this month's sales figures, make a simple table showing this month's sales figures – don't spend an entire morning
creating beautiful graphs that display all the figures for
this year.

# Moving from Reactive to Proactive

When you find you're rushing around like the proverbial head-
less chicken, the chances are that you're probably reacting to
a situation. When an email comes into your inbox, you react
and feel compelled to do something with it. When the phone
rings, you feel the urge to answer it. When someone asks you
to do something, you feel the need to respond.

## Managing deadlines

Deadlines are great for providing focus and creating a sense of urgency when working on a task. However, deadlines can be a major source of stress when they become unrealistic.

Managing other people's expectations is one way of getting back in control of your time. If someone sets you an unmanageable deadline, say no (see the section 'Just Saying "No"') or go back and renegotiate the deadline.

Remember that other people's deadlines are nearly always *not* your problem. Just because someone isn't as organised as you, doesn't mean you have to drop everything. Remember your boundaries.

Equally, don't make your sense of urgency someone else's problem. Plan ahead, building in leeway, and don't leave things to the last minute.

Start being proactive and take better control of your time. You don't have to say 'how high?' every time someone says 'jump'. Look ahead and use planning as a way of taking control. Plan when you're going to answer your emails, plan when you're going to deal with your phone calls, and take some time to think about whether you can or want to do what someone asks.

Look at the big picture and use goal setting (see Chapter 1) to plan your time. Using you goal setting plan makes you less reactive and more in control.

Quite often you may find yourself spending time worrying about things over which you actually have no control. Don't. There's no point in wasting your time and energy. If you can't do anything about a certain situation then just focus on what you can do. For example, you may not have any control or responsibility for what another department does, but you can control the work you do.

# *Just Saying 'No'*

Never mind 'sorry' being the hardest word, 'no' can be equally hard to say. Especially if you're the sort of person who's eager to please and wants to help. Many busy people are busy because they just don't know when to say no.

The following sections reassure you that 'no' is a perfectly valid and reasonable response sometimes, and show you how to use this tiny word as a valuable time management tool.

Your time is an important and limited commodity. If you said yes to every request for money, you'd soon be broke. The same goes for your time.

## Recognising the consequences of saying yes

You're likely so used to saying yes, or being expected to say yes, because it's rude or you may upset someone by saying no, that you do it automatically without really thinking. Some people nearly always say yes to those in authority – your parents (unless you're a terrible two or a reluctant teenager), your boss, and leaders in business or in your community.

But the more you say yes, the more people ask you to do even more. And if you keep saying yes, you end up taking on more and more and, in the end, something's gotta give.

Sometimes saying yes just seems easier – it saves the hassle of having an argument, of having to give a reason for not doing it, or feeling guilty if you say no. Anyway, you're sure that you can fit it in somewhere. You might be able to, but saying yes always has consequences:

- ✔ You end up working late in order to finish all the extra work you've taken on.

- ✔ You have to rush things through to get everything done.

- ✔ You end up dropping something (literally or metaphorically) and letting someone down.

- ✔ You can't put the same amount of time and effort into one of your many projects and the quality suffers because you do a half-hearted job.

- ✔ You miss out on doing something you'd rather be doing because you've already said yes to something else.

✔ You end up with no free time because every minute is crammed full of all those things you've said yes to.

✔ You end up being ill because your body is saying no (frequent colds, stomach bugs, or aches and pains are an indication that you're taking on too much – take a look at Chapter 15 to remedy these ills).

When you say yes to something you're making a commitment with your time and that means something has to give. Time is limited to 24 hours in a day. Every minute of every day you're doing something, whether it's at work, home, relaxing, socialising, or sleeping. If you want to fit in an activity, then you carve time out from a different part of your day. If you've got some spare capacity then that's not a problem. However, if you're already doing too many things, then you can end up sacrificing precious time from positive activities like resting and spending time with family and friends.

So when someone asks you to do something, think carefully about where a 'yes' response might lead. Be realistic about what you're able to achieve. You can't say yes to everything without crumbling under the weight of responsibility, time constraints, or the shear volume of work.

## Making the yes/no decision

Don't say yes until you know exactly what it is you're agreeing to and what you're taking on. What may appear to be a five-minute job or just an hourly commitment once a month can quite easily turn into something a lot bigger. That request to join the PTA, help out at the local fun run, join a special interest group, signup for an evening class, join the gym, work on a new project, and so on – it all takes time.

Ask yourself the following questions:

✔ **What does the request involve?** Make sure that you know exactly what's what before you agree to anything.

✔ **How much of my time will this take?** If you're already familiar with the task, then you have an idea of how long it might take. If you're working on something new to you it takes longer the first few times. And don't forget all the extra demands on your time a task may bring – for example, doing a two-hour presentation involves time to prepare, travel, and follow up.

✔ **What will I lose?** If you say yes, what are you also saying no to? For example, By saying yes to finishing an urgent report by the end of the day, you're saying no to finishing work on time. By saying yes to taking on a piece of additional work or participating in a new project, you're saying no to having time for yourself, your children/partner/friends.

✔ **Do I want to do this task?** Am I interested and motivated? Life is about choices and the way you manage your time is no different. You always have a choice in deciding what you're going to do in any given moment. Base your decision on the expected benefits or consequences, and how these tie in with what you want.

✔ **Do I *really* have time?** The bottom line: do you have the capacity to do this task?

Some people delight in shifting goalposts around. Don't let them do that to you! Lay down your limits at the start of a task, and then stick to them. If someone tells you he only needs a day of your time, then make sure that's what he gets. If you do decide to re-negotiate, go back to the start and ask yourself these four questions again.

Give yourself 24 hours to think over any new request for your time. If you've got caught up in the moment, these 24 hours allow any over enthusiasm to die down and for reality to kick in when you consult your diary and see that you really don't have any time available.

## Using the 'no' word effectively

The more you say no, the easier it becomes and the more in control you are of your own time.

Be upfront and honest with people and they won't think any less of you for saying no. Better to say no now than let people down by saying yes and then no at a later date.

### Looking at ways to say no

You don't have to come out with an outright 'No'. You can say no without seeming harsh or ungrateful.

✔ 'I'm so glad you asked but I'm too busy to do that right now.'

✔ 'I don't have my diary with me. Can I get back to you later?'

✔ 'Thank you for asking but I'm not interested.'

✔ 'I'm not able to do that but perhaps John may be able to help.'

✔ 'Can I let you know tomorrow?'

✔ 'Thank you for the invitation but it's the only time I have free this week, so I have to say no.'

✔ 'We'd love to go away but we already have plans for that weekend.'

Don't make elaborate excuses or go into long explanations of why you're saying no, there's no need to. A simple 'because' suffices – 'I can't come to your party because I have to work that evening.'

You don't have to say no and leave it at that. If you want to be helpful, why not pass the opportunity on to someone else or find a compromise? You can't do that job now, but you know someone who can. Or perhaps you don't have time to do everything, but you do have a couple of hours in which you can help out.

### Knowing that no means no

Say 'No' clearly, and mean it. When it comes down to it, your time is yours and it's your choice as to how you spend it. Don't be misled by other people's expectations – whether that's family, friends, even your boss or work colleagues.

Don't be tempted to replace a no with a maybe. You're just putting off making a clear decision or avoiding making a commitment. Saying maybe when what you actually mean is no isn't fair on the other person, who may well think maybe means yes.

### Practising saying no

If saying no is a challenge for you or you've a particular situation that you feel is going to be awkward or uncomfortable because you need to say no, you may want to practice with a friend or colleague. Get comfortable with being able to say no in as many different ways as possible and think about different reactions. What's the worst that can happen? What's a person's likely reaction?

If you really want to hone your 'saying no' skill, have a bit of fun and spend the whole of the next week saying no. You might find this uncomfortable to start with or feel that you're missing out on something, but try it.

---

# Scaling the 'I wish I'd said no' mountain

Oops. You've failed miserably at saying no recently, and now you're standing at the bottom of a gigantic mountain of work and other commitments, wondering how you'll ever reach the summit. What now?

Well first, recognise that you've failed to set clear boundaries and to say no when it was appropriate. Take a look at the section 'Just Saying "No"' and work on your nay-saying ability.

Next, you need to tackle the mountain:

✓ **Prioritise:** You've got too much on your plate, so something has to give. What's it going to be? Take a look at all your existing projects, tasks, roles, and decide which are important to you and which aren't. Use the prioritising technique from Chapter 4 to help you.

✓ **Delegate:** Can you reduce your workload by giving tasks to someone else? Chapter 11 has lots of info on how to delegate.

✓ **Focus:** Are you able to apply the 80/20 rule (refer to Chapter 2) and do less work to achieve the same result? The rule states that 80 per cent of the results can be achieved with 20 per cent of the effort or by doing 20 per cent of the work. Do the important things first that give you the greatest result or have the biggest impact.

✓ **Renegotiate:** Talk to your boss, colleagues or clients, admit you're very busy, and see whether you can adjust the time-frame or the amount of work required.

# Part III
# Organising the Work You Do

"Aaaargh!!– emails, answer phones,
fax machines and now even the alphabet
soup is sending me messages."

## *In this part . . .*

**G**ood time management depends on having a system to deal with the things you need to do each day. In these chapters you find ways to deal with everyday challenges such as meetings, emails, and paperwork. I explain how to deal with interruptions effectively and politely. If you really want to get more done, find out how you can maximise your time by getting other people involved.

# Chapter 6

# Making the Most of Meetings

- - - - - - - - - - - - - - - - - - - - - - - - - - - - - - - - - - -

### In This Chapter

▶ Looking at different types of meeting

▶ Keeping the meeting organised

▶ Making sure that the meeting runs smoothly

▶ Scheduling your journey to the meeting

▶ Getting into networking

- - - - - - - - - - - - - - - - - - - - - - - - - - - - - - - - - - -

*M*eetings can be a great way of keeping track of projects, reviewing progress, solving problems, and discussing new opportunities. Meetings can include seminars, workshops, training, and any situation where more than one person is gathered in one room.

However, some meetings can be real time-wasters. This chapter guides you towards making the most of meetings and avoiding wasting time.

## Do We Really Need Another Meeting?

Before arranging or attending a meeting, consider whether it's the most effective use of everybody's time. Can the information be communicated by email or a written report? What do you actually want to get out of the meeting? Meetings need to be relevant and appropriate. Don't hold a meeting just for the sake of it and don't attend a meeting unless it's relevant to you. If in doubt, ask.

## The statistics say it all

Studies show that ineffective meetings lead to general dissatisfaction and an increase in employee turnover. Badly run and ineffective meetings are listed as one of the top three timewasters and are the reason that 70 per cent of employees feel that they're unproductive.

Holding a meeting means that a number of people spend a certain amount of their limited time in one place. The result can be a loss of productivity if the meeting is unhelpful. The outcome of the meeting should at least go some way to balance the input of time and effort.

# Choosing the Right Type of Meeting

If you're organising the meeting, decide on the type of meeting you need. People don't necessarily have to be in the same room in order to meet. These days teleconferencing and web conferencing can be arranged (see the later section 'Tele/Web conferences' for details) and can save a huge amount of time and money in travel when several people, or large distances, are involved.

## Face to face

If you're working in a team, face-to-face meetings can be useful. If you all work in the same office, or within a short distance from each other, a face-to-face meeting is easy to arrange.

If you're part of a work team that's located in different offices or even different countries, then organising a face-to-face meeting may be difficult. However, such meetings still need to happen in order to help team members gel with each other. Although meetings held over the phone can work, meeting face to face may be the only chance that people can get to know other members of the team.

# Tele/Web conferences

Teleconferences or web conferences enable people to meet and discuss key objectives without having to be in the same room or even the same country. Teleconferences are held as a live group call over the phone, using speakerphones at each end of the line, with or without the use of video cameras. Web conferences take place over the Internet with the use of a broadband phone connection and web cam.

Setting up team project meetings or training sessions using group conference call facilities, or over the Internet, is easy. These teleconferences can include presentations and notes online in 'classroom' format. Everyone is able to share notes and write up comments on the screen without being physically present.

Group teleconference calls don't allow for any visual cues so you need to handle these meetings carefully to ensure that everyone gets a chance to speak, that you document key points, and make follow-up actions clear.

 Test out any technology ahead of time, perhaps doing a dry run first, to make sure that it works – you can iron out any hiccups before the actual meeting.

# Planning the Meeting

When it's your responsibility to organise the meeting, before you even start arranging it, think about what you hope to achieve and put your objectives down in writing. For example: 'As a result of this meeting I want to clarify the next steps for the project' or 'come up with a solution to the current problem'.

You need to know why you're meeting and that you're involving the right people. A successful meeting depends on selecting only the people who need to be there to achieve the overall objective.

Think carefully about who needs to be involved in the meeting when making decisions or providing the right information. Remember these considerations when planning a meeting:

✔ Don't invite people unnecessarily – you're just wasting their time if they don't really need to be there.

✔ Don't invite two people with the same roles if only one person is needed to provide the information or make decisions.

✔ Give people enough notice. Don't expect people to be able to attend at the drop of a hat – unless it's a real emergency. You can give a couple of days' notice for an in-house, project-based meeting or a few months for a full-day meeting, workshop, or training session. The key to managing your own, and everyone else's, time is planning – particularly when it comes to meetings.

✔ Decide on a suitable location, how long the meeting needs to be, and, most importantly, have an agenda (I cover agendas in the next section).

✔ Confirm things ahead of time such as the meeting venue, attendees, speakers, agenda, equipment, and hand-outs. Create a checklist so that you know everything is covered and confirm all final arrangements with attendees a couple of days before.

✔ Get to the venue or meeting room in good time on the actual day to check everything out.

✔ Have a plan B in case certain key people don't turn up, or something goes wrong, or isn't working. Decide at what point it's necessary to cancel the meeting.

If you need to have a large meeting or event, get a professional event organiser involved to deal with all the logistics and to free you up to focus on other aspects of the meeting – such as the attendees and content.

# Running the Meeting

If a meeting is going to be effective, you need to run it properly.

## Agendas

*All* meetings need an agenda, no matter how big or small, short or long the meeting is. An agenda helps to keep the meeting on track and to time.

## Tips for meetings

Some useful guidelines for meetings are:

✔ Be on time

✔ Be respectful towards other delegates

✔ Define roles and responsibilities

✔ Get involved – don't sit on the sidelines

✔ Stay focused and keep to the agenda

✔ Maintain confidentiality

✔ Agree actions and next steps

The agenda needs to include the start time, end time, and objectives and outcomes for the meeting. Send it out to everyone that's due to attend ahead of time as soon as you confirm the date (or at least a week beforehand), so people have time to prepare. If additional information is required send it out with the agenda. If you need people to bring information to the meeting or carry out any pre-work, make this clear in the agenda. Sending an agenda out also enables you to check that everyone's still able to make it.

If you're organising a workshop or seminar, people want to know the agenda in advance or at least have an overview in order to decide whether to attend.

Start on time. Even if you have a few latecomers, don't let them delay things. Don't try to cram too much into a meeting. Keep on track. The person responsible for running the meeting needs to keep to the agenda, keep to time, and bring people back on track if they go off on a tangent. Make sure that everyone gets a chance to speak, and don't let one person dominate the meeting. Leave time at the beginning and end of the meeting for introductions, discussing the agenda, and summarising the agreed follow-up actions. Always let people know when the meeting is due to finish and don't allow meetings to over-run.

Have a few optional items or discussion points on the agenda. If you're running over, you can omit the optional extras.

Allow time for breaks and refreshments. If it's a full day's meeting don't forget that you need to provide lunch or have an appropriate break for people to get their own.

At the end of the meeting agree on the next date to meet if you need a follow-up meeting. Fixing a date with everyone in the same room is easier than spending time chasing people up afterwards.

## *Taking notes*

If you need to keep a record of the meeting delegate someone to take notes (or *minutes*). Depending on the type of meeting these can be formal or informal notes. If you hold regular meetings then create a template that can be used at each one thus saving time typing up the same information each time. Notes for board meetings always need a formal structure (including the date, location, and what was discussed) because these need to be kept on record.

Create handouts for the meeting to share information. Flip charts can be really useful for noting down key points, brain-storming, and capturing key actions, and can then be used to type up the notes.

Any follow-up actions coming out of the meeting need to be properly minuted with the specific action, agreed dates, and responsibilities noted.

Send out the follow-up notes as soon as possible after the meeting – certainly within a couple of days – so that any actions can be dealt with. If you need confirmation or approval of any meeting minutes or notes send out a draft first, and send the final copy after any comments or changes have been made.

If you've come away with an armful of handouts and leaflets, as soon as you get back to the office sort them into the four categories I discuss in Chapter 7:

- ✔ Action
- ✔ Read
- ✔ File
- ✔ Bin

Don't dump the handouts into the 'leave it for later' pile – you know what happens to that!

If you agreed to do something or contact someone at a later date, put a note in your diary.

Get feedback after the meeting. Feedback provides valuable information for planning future meetings and helps you to see if the meeting met the planned objectives. Hand out a feedback form as part of the meeting agenda or follow-up with attendees after the meeting.

# Getting to Your Meetings on Time

How often do you arrive late for a meeting or find yourself rushing to arrive just in the nick of time? You can ensure that you always arrive on time for your meetings by planning sufficient time at either end.

Aim to arrive a few minutes early even for in-house or local meetings. Respect the organiser and the other attendees. Arriving early means you have a few minutes to settle yourself in and prepare what you need to say. (For strategies for dealing with 'spare time' see Chapter 17).

## Calculating travel time

If you need to travel to a meeting, start by planning backwards from your scheduled arrival time. Aim to arrive at least five to ten minutes early if the meeting is less than an hour away – whether that's on foot, by bus, train, or car.

When road or rail travel is involved you don't know what unexpected delays may occur. Delays can include heavy traffic, stopping for petrol, queues at ticket offices, and leaves on the line!

Travelling during peak commuting times means busier roads, and packed buses and trains. Longer travel times need more leeway at either end.

Don't forget to allow extra time either side of the actual journey time for parking and actually getting to the meeting.

Many training and networking meetings usually have a half-hour time slot for registration. However, don't assume that if registration starts at 9.30 a.m. and the meeting starts at 10.00 a.m. you can arrive at 9.55 a.m.! Aim to arrive for 9.30 a.m. By the time you've parked, walked to the location, found where you're meant to be, registered, and got a cup of coffee it's probably 9.45 a.m. You now have time to talk to the other people before settling down, relaxed, and ready to start.

If you're taking the bus or train aim to catch an earlier one than you need. If you happen to miss that, you know that you've still got plan B: the second train or bus that will still get you there on time.

Don't aim to go for plan B before you've even started. It's there in case you're delayed in getting to the station or catching a bus.

## Leaving in good time

Don't stress yourself out before you even begin heading off to a meeting. Make sure that you set off for your meeting in good time. If it takes you an hour to drive to the location of the meeting, leave ten minutes early.

Even if you have lots to do before you leave, don't leave things to the last minute. Give yourself a good five or ten minutes to get out of the house or office and on your journey. It may take you that long to gather all your papers together, find your keys, switch on the answer machine, find your mobile, and so on.

If you have an early start the following day, get out everything you need the night before. Put everything in your briefcase or bag that you need for the meeting ahead of time. That way you can get up and go without rushing around at the last minute.

# Networking Meetings

Business owners attend networking meetings and here you have the opportunity to talk to your colleagues and peers, develop alliances, and build your business and relationships.

The meetings are often held over breakfast, so you still have a full day at work, or in the early evening so you can go straight from the office.

Hundreds of different networking groups meet around the country aimed at different types of business from small to large. More women-only networks are springing up aimed at busy working mums, so they can juggle networking with the demands of children and family.

Find a networking meeting near you by visiting:

- ✔ Business Networking International: `www.bni-europe.com/uk/`

- ✔ Business Referral Exchange: `www.brxnet.co.uk`

- ✔ Networking for women in business: `www.theathenanetwork.com`

- ✔ Local Chambers of Commerce: `www.chamberonline.co.uk`

- ✔ Contact me at `www.clareevans.co.uk` for my information sheet on networking groups around the country.

Make sure that the events you attend relate to your business. If possible get a list of potential attendees before you arrive, so you have an idea of who's going to be there and who you want to talk to, which saves time when you get there.

If you regularly attend networking events, think about what you plan to get from the proceedings to make sure that it's an effective use of your time, such as:

- ✔ Meeting new contacts.

- ✔ Getting new ideas.

- ✔ Brainstorming with colleagues.

- ✔ Finding out about new developments.

- ✔ Developing existing relationships.

- ✔ Finding suppliers.

- ✔ Growing your business.

Networking meetings aren't about doing business. No one likes to have a sales pitch in the first few minutes of meeting you. Networking is about making connections and building relationships.

Don't give out your business card to anyone and everyone – only do so if you're asked for it and if it's relevant. Equally, don't automatically collect cards for the sake of it.

Enter the useful business cards into your contact system as soon as possible when you get back to the office. Include the date and place that you met and any relevant notes about the person and his or her business.

Send a follow-up email or phone your new contact within a couple of days of the meeting to continue your initial discussion or arrange a subsequent meeting. Add the person to your mailing list so you can keep in touch.

# Chapter 7

# Saving Time by Organising Your Paperwork

*D*ealing with paperwork is one of those things that you just can't avoid. Despite the fact that the personal computer was supposed to replace the need for paper, the reality is that it hasn't. In fact, with photocopiers, faxes, and people printing out emails, paperwork has probably increased.

Whether at home or at work, people still like to read hard copy. Paper is never going to disappear. There's nothing quite like holding a piece of paper in your hand. It's easier to read and more portable than lugging your laptop around or squinting at your mobile phone screen.

Tackling your paperwork can seem overwhelming. You find paper and receipts lurking in piles around the house, in your office, stuffed into drawers, and hiding away in boxes. Fear not – this chapter shows you systems to get your paperwork under control and help you to keep it that way – which will do wonders for your time management!

## Getting Started

Sorting your paperwork starts with a modest spending spree. Go out and buy as many folders, trays, boxes, and files as you need to organise your papers. It'll pay off in the long run, saving you time by no longer hunting through stacks of papers looking for that one important memo you need to finish the task at hand.

## Writing your shopping list

Here are a few useful items you may want to consider buying if you don't have an existing supply:

✔ A4/Foolscap square cut folders for organising and sorting paperwork in your filing system.

✔ Ring binders and lever arch files for loose sheets of paper, client files, and accounts.

✔ Expanding folders/project files labelled A–Z, or 1–12 and so on – useful for filing invoices and receipts for your accounts.

✔ Stacking filing trays to save space on your desk.

✔ Hanging files for your filing cabinet.

✔ Coloured permanent pens.

✔ Labels of various sizes and colours.

✔ Hole-punch.

✔ Clear plastic punched pockets to use in ring binders.

✔ Coloured plastic folders (it's easy to find your tax info if it's in a red folder).

✔ Dividers either numbered, or with the month or day.

✔ Envelopes.

You can store ring binders and lever arch files on shelves to keep frequently used paperwork easily to hand.

When buying stationery items, buy two of each. Don't waste time searching when one of them goes astray. People are always borrowing (and then not bringing back) things like scissors for example, which are useful in many situations around the home and office.

## *Getting in file*

Getting your paperwork filed away is important if you don't want it cluttering up your home or office. Some sort of system is essential if you want to be able to retrieve information after you've filed it.

The filing cabinet is an essential piece of furniture for every office, to store away and organise your paperwork. If you don't already have a filing system, put one together as soon as possible.

A simple two-drawer filing cabinet with hanging files and a series of card folders, appropriately labelled, can suffice. Make sure that you get enough folders, tabs, and labels to mark up all the files as you go and always have a few spare for when you need to make new file.

Bookshelves are ideal for storing folders, files and ring binders – as well as the books and items that you readily need to hand.

Use folders to organise your work in both the virtual world as well as the paper-based world. You waste less time searching if you're well organised.

Create folders in your email system and document folders that match the paper folders in your office (check out Chapter10 for more info). Doing so makes it easier to find and retrieve information from both your electronic system and your paper-based system.

Be careful with your naming conventions – use titles that actually mean something. Will you actually remember in six months' time what the file you called 'Fred's Stuff' actually means or what it contains? Save yourself time and keep naming simple.

Keep separate files or folders for action items, your accounts, tax information, client information, invoices, reading material, household bills, insurance, and your car documents. Separating out your paperwork saves you from wasting time hunting down information you need. Follow these tips:

✔ **Colourful plastic folders** are great for sorting paperwork and if you have all your tax information or accounts in a red file, easier to find too.

✔ **Clear plastic pockets** are useful for sorting loose articles from magazines.

✔ **Ring binders** are handy for accounts, articles, client information – anything you need sorted and to hand.

✔ **Envelopes** are ideal for storing receipts, vouchers, tickets, and small scraps of paper you want to keep. Label the envelopes appropriately and file them where you won't lose them!

✔ **Magazine holders** are solid containers made of plastic, cardboard, or metal that fit on a bookshelf. You can use them for storing loose magazines upright, as well as slotting several folders in one place.

# Climbing on Top of Paperwork

The well-known golden rule to dealing with paper is to do something with it the first time you touch it. I don't hold with the 'handle it only once' rule, because this system doesn't really work in practice. However, if you can avoid shuffling paperwork from one pile to another you certainly waste less time and work more efficiently.

Paperwork tends to accumulate because you don't know what to do with it so you put it to one side – just in case. All those 'hmmm, not sure what to do with this' bits of paper end up in piles that simply grow as you add to them.

Get rid of all those little bits of paper that you stuff into pockets, bags, and drawers. Carry a notebook with you and use it to write everything down in one place – all those telephone numbers, addresses, and notes from meetings.

When the post lands on your doormat or as paperwork comes into your office, decide what to do with it there and then. Be ruthless. Put the paperwork straight into the appropriate file, tray, or folder – Action, Read, File, or Bin (see the following sections).

Keep the waste bin, shredder, or recycling box next to you so you don't have a pile of wastepaper waiting to be binned.

## Action

Your large A4 Action folder is for paperwork that you need to take action on such as bills to pay, calls to make, appointments to book, forms to be completed, and documents to sign.

If you want to break down the Action folder still further, you can sub-divide the folder into several sections for bills, phone calls, clients and so on, and put the paper in the appropriate place. All you need to do is to go to this one place to find what you need.

Deal with the Action items immediately or as soon as possible at the time you've planned to deal with them. For example, you can choose to pay your bills on a particular day of the week and make your calls in the morning.

## Read

Your Read folder is for letters, magazines, reports, or newsletters to read later. Again, subdividing this folder into files such as Review, Business, and Fun can save time when you're trying to locate things.

Set aside time in your week for reading, such as a break at lunchtime or at the end of the week.

Cut out interesting articles and keep them in your Read folder for reference but clear the folder out once a year to keep it manageable. If an article has remained in your unread pile for a long period of time, chuck it out. Cancel any magazines that you don't have time to read any more.

Grab your Read folder to take with you for those quiet moments when you're sitting waiting for a meeting and have a few moments to spare.

## File

Your File folder is for statements, receipts, and articles that you've dealt with but need to keep.

File receipts and accounts information in their own folder so that you can deal with them easily when you're working on your accounts (see 'Storing Important Documents and Data' later in this chapter). You don't need to deal with your accounts information immediately. However, this information tends to build up so it needs careful attention when filing so that it's not in a complete mess when you need it.

When you file your paperwork, check for any documents that you can now take out and throw away. For example, if you're filing your new insurance document, throw the old one away. Be sure to keep any important financial and tax info for seven years before you throw it out.

## Bin

You guessed it: the Bin category is for all that junk mail, flyers, and paperwork that you've dealt with and no longer need. Add these to the recycling pile as soon as you receive them. Don't be tempted to hang onto something 'just in case'. Be realistic – how often do you refer back to papers that you've carefully put to one side or stuck in a drawer.

Save scrap paper and the reverse of junk mail for printing off drafts and writing lists.

## Reviewing your system once in a while

If after a few months you find parts of your system aren't working – change them. If you don't like using folders, put paperwork in trays on your desk rather than tucked away in your filing cabinet or drawer. Write things out if you prefer not to use the computer – or vice versa.

What's more intuitive for you – filing things alphabetically or by date? Do you prefer to have everything out and easily to hand or tucked away out of sight? There's no right or wrong answer – just what works best for you. You only get control of your paperwork if you have a system that works for you and makes sense for the way that you work.

Organising your paperwork doesn't mean that you have to operate a clear desk policy or never have a single piece of paper on view. You can use the trays, folders, and files in a way that works best for you. If you can't a find the piece of paper that you're looking for within a few minutes, your existing system needs to change.

 One of the biggest time-saving strategies with paperwork is 'little and often'. If you can get into the habit of organising your paperwork as you go, you not only avoid the stress of having to do it all in one go, but also the need to set aside a large chunk of time to do it.

# Reducing the Incoming Flood

By checking what's coming in on a regular basis, you can reduce the amount of paper that comes through your door or into your office in the first place, thereby saving yourself time.

Most statements and bills are now available online. Store them electronically or print them off if you need them. Get as much paperwork as you can electronically.

Cancel subscriptions to newspapers or magazines that you no longer need. Read magazines and newspapers online or at your local library. Most publications with a website publish their most recent articles online. Newspaper sites have searchable archives. You can also recycle old magazines by taking them to your local library, hospital, or doctors' surgery.

Cancel all those catalogues that you get sent on a regular basis, just because you ordered something two years ago.

 Subscribe to the Mailing Preference Service (MPS) by visiting www.mpsonline.org.uk to avoid unnecessary junk mail coming through your door. After a couple of months you should see a significant drop in unsolicited mail.

Remember to tick the box on forms that prevents the company from sending you promotional mail or your address being sent to third parties. Find the little checkbox in the small print at the bottom of the form. Check the small print carefully in case you need to tick the box if you *do* want to receive mail.

Never fill in those shopping surveys or forms offering a prize draw. The chances are you'll be added to a mailing list and receive even more junk mail. The same goes for free samples that require you to give your address. There's no such thing as a 'free' sample!

# Clearing a Backlog

Sometimes you may need to tackle a BIG filing pile. If you have a large pile of filing or several piles taking up space on your desk, in your office, or around the house, set aside a couple of hours in your diary when you're going to have time to deal with it.

Set aside time at the end of the day or, if you need to clear a big backlog at home, perhaps at a weekend or even one evening. (This is a one-time job to clear a big backlog. I want to reduce your hours of work and chores – not extend them!) Follow these steps:

1. **Gather all your papers into one big pile or put them all into one box.** Go through the pile one by one and sort each piece of paper into sub-piles of Action, Read, File, and Bin (refer to the previous section if you need a reminder).

   Don't forget to look in those other places where paper can accumulate – bags, briefcases, and the car.

2. **Action anything that's lurking.** Put to one side anything that you need to read. Bin anything you no longer need (it's amazing how if you hold onto a piece of paper long enough, suddenly it doesn't become important any more and you can quite happily throw it away).

3. **File the rest.** You may end up surrounded by several piles of bank statements, credit cards statements, client info, paid invoices and so on but at least you can now pick them up together and file them in one go.

In just a couple of hours you've reduced your paperwork mountain into a few paper hillocks. The large pile of paperwork that's been taunting you for months is now several small piles that can be filed away and one pile that can go straight into the bin. How satisfying is that?

A few hours should be all you need, even for a large pile. If you can't file it all away in one hit, do what you can in the time you have and make an effort to clear a little bit each day. Give yourself a time limit to get it all cleared. You'll be amazed how quickly it disappears when you put your mind to it.

 Put on your favourite music, set a time limit, and clearing your paperwork won't seem like such a chore. Even better, run this exercise as part of a Focus Day (refer to Chapter 2)

# Storing Important Documents and Data

Losing important documents or data can jeopardise your business or your financial security, to say nothing of wasting time searching for them or getting them replaced. Make sure that you have a Plan B in place in case such an event occurs.

## Looking after your documents

Keep important documents in a safe at home or in a safe deposit box in your local bank. Make two lists of the documents and keep one in the envelope that you leave with the bank and keep one at home for reference. Don't forget to update your list if you add something in or take anything out. Most banks only charge a minimal annual amount to keep an A4 envelope – unless you need regular access.

✔ **Bank Statements.** Order these by account number and date. Keep in a ring binder for the current year and archive previous years' statements in storage boxes.

✔ **Personal Documents.** You don't need birth and marriage certificates, mortgage agreements, and wills on a regular basis so place them in safe storage with your bank or solicitor, or in a safe at home.

✔ **Share Certificates.** If you have paper certificates, keep them safe and keep a record of the important details such as shareholder ID and number of shares.

✔ **Passports and ID cards.** You often need these on a regular basis, so keep them somewhere safe in the house and where you won't forget where they are when you're packing for your holiday.

Shred anything you don't need that has personal information and your address on it such as bank details and utility bills.

## Holding on to your data

Whether held electronically or on paper your data, such as customer records, letters, orders, costs, and so on, is essential to you and to your business. Make sure that you keep at least two electronic copies of all essential data, one copy of which is stored in a safe environment. In the event of a disaster such as a fire you must be able to recover all the important information and data. See the sidebar 'Staying on the safe side: Backups' for info on backing up electronic files.

### Staying on the safe side: Backups

Back up your data – particularly files and information you have on your computer. If you lost your hard drive (it does happen!) how would you recover your data? What would the impact be?

Here are some ways you can protect yourself from the damaging impact of a technology breakdown:

✔ **Back up onto external devices:** Make sure that you copy your important files and contact details to an external source. You can use CDs or DVDs, or USB pens (see Chapter 18). Alternatively, external hard drives provide additional storage capacity for documents, photos, and music files that attach to your computer via the USB port or a separate cable connection. They are a low-cost solution (£50–£100) – especially when you consider the cost of losing your data. Most of them just plug into your computer and automatically run a regular backup of your hard drive.

✔ **Use an online backup facility:** Online backup is available over a broadband connection. Software is installed on your computer and your data is backed up to a server at a secure location somewhere else. Use a search engine such as Google for free online backup packages that back up a limited amount of data. Alternatively, you can pay companies to have a larger storage capacity, and then back up your whole hard drive. In the event of a computer failure or loss of data it can be restored and get you back up and running.

✔ **Synchronise your computer with a PDA/Blackberry or mobile phone:** This keeps your calendar, contacts, and email up-to-date.

✔ **Use an online mail system:** At least you can temporarily access your email. Most local libraries offer free Internet access to check your email.

✔ **Keep a note of your usernames and passwords:** Write them down in coded form so that it's not obvious to the casual observer. Never store what you've written near your computer (such as on sticky notes) or carry it with you in wallets and purses. And *never* write down passwords to financial data – you need to rely on the old grey matter to remember these!

✔ **Keep everything to do with the software you use:** Without a list of which applications you use – as well as any original discs, downloadable files, and serial numbers or access codes – how can you get back up and running if your computer crashes?

✔ **Protect yourself from corruptions and viruses:** Install software updates and make sure that your computer is running up-to-date virus software.

✔ **Test your backup every now and then:** Don't just check the log file, restore the data. Nothing's worse than sitting back feeling smug and thinking your data is being safely backed up only to find out, when you actually need it, that it's not!

# Keeping Your Accounts

Keeping your accounts uptodate and organised can be one of the biggest sources of paperwork, particularly if you work from home or run your own business.

Even if you hate doing your accounts, having a system for sorting your paperwork makes things easier to deal with, saves you time, and you won't lose vital bits of information.

Get an expanding file – one with dividers for each month is useful. Alternatively, an A4 ring binder or lever arch file will do. As your receipts, invoices, and statements come in, and as the bills are paid, put them straight into the appropriate section each month. Keep loose receipts and the smaller bits of paper in a plastic pocket.

Everything you need is in one place so that updating your accounts system at the end of the month, or preferably each week (little and often!), is easy. Or just hand the entire file/folder to your accountant or bookkeeper.

After your monthly accounts have been done, file the documents in the appropriate place.

# Tackling the End of Year Clearout

Sort through your filing system at least once a year or every six months. Get rid of old, expired paperwork, and anything else you no longer need.

Move any important paperwork you still need to keep into storage boxes and put it into storage (or the loft if you're at home) so it's not taking up space in your filing cabinet. Financial and tax related documents should be kept for six years – especially if they relate to your business.

# Chapter 8

# Dealing with Your Emails

● ● ● ● ● ● ● ● ● ● ● ● ● ● ● ● ● ● ● ● ● ● ● ● ● ● ● ● ● ● ● ● ● ● ● ● ● ● ● ● ● ● ●

*In This Chapter*

▶ Knowing when to check your messages

▶ Getting control of your inbox

▶ Organising your emails

▶ Handling a backlog

● ● ● ● ● ● ● ● ● ● ● ● ● ● ● ● ● ● ● ● ● ● ● ● ● ● ● ● ● ● ● ● ● ● ● ● ● ● ● ● ● ● ●

*M*odern technology is designed to make our lives easier and to make us more productive. Email is a great way to communicate with people around the world, easily, effectively, and more quickly than the traditional methods of communication. However, emails need to be handled sensibly, so that they don't become something else that sucks up your time.

In this chapter, I take you through setting up a smooth, efficient email-processing system – from deciding when to check emails and using tools and techniques to manage messages, to dealing with the inevitable backlogs that build up when you take a break from work.

## *Dedicating Time to Your Emails*

Do you constantly check your inbox for new messages throughout the day? When you hear the email alert go, do you switch from whatever you're doing and go and check the latest message?

Emails can be a great time waster and provide a constant distraction throughout the day. If you're going to make the most of your day then one way to increase your productivity is to manage the amount of time you spend on emails.

## Checking your email periodically

Only check your emails every so often throughout the day –
perhaps first thing, late morning, and again in the afternoon.

Set your email system to only check for new messages period-
ically (say every two hours or so) or disconnect yourself from
the Internet except when you want to download emails. In
most applications you can change the settings by clicking
Tools on the top menu, and then Settings.

Emails are rarely so urgent that you need to respond to them
immediately, unless an instant response is expected as part of
your job.

## Setting aside time for emails

If you need to spend time responding to emails, set aside time
in your schedule to do that and make sure that you put a limit
on the amount of time you spend, otherwise you're likely to
end up distracted and sidetracked, and spending more time
than you intended.

When you're on 'email time', don't jump straight in and start
responding to the first one, unless you have only a few new
messages. If you have more messages than you can comfortably deal with in half an hour or so, take a few minutes to scan
through and sort them into urgent/action, non-urgent, and
reading.

Limit yourself to 30 minutes at a time, or work to clear the
existing action emails for as long as it takes (within reason!)
without addressing any new emails. Leave those until next time.

You must factor in the expectations and needs of your clients,
customers, and/or colleagues. How quickly do you really need
to respond to emails? Does your work require you to respond
immediately or can you wait a few hours or maybe even until
the next day? If an email requires a lengthy response, send a
confirmation email to let the sender know that you've received
her email and will reply shortly.

# *Managing Your Inbox*

Find a way to control your inbox and you'll find it a lot easier to manage the volume of email that comes in on a daily basis. Use various systems and tools and your inbox won't become such an overwhelming source of stress and frustration. Create good mail-handling habits so you have more time available.

## *Organising your incoming mail*

Being organised is the key to time-efficient email processing. Here are some simple things you can do to sort your new messages quickly and easily.

### *Setting up folders*

Filters and folders can be very useful tools in helping you to manage your inbox. Just like paper filing, you categorise your emails, which helps you prioritise them and easily see what actions you need to take.

To start off with, create the following folders:

- ✔ Action
- ✔ Newsletters
- ✔ Priority
- ✔ Reading
- ✔ Reference

Then make additional folders for specific projects or clients.

### *Filtering emails*

After you set up your folders, you can introduce filters in your mail program that automatically sort your incoming mail into the correct folder, making it quicker and easier to deal with your inbox.

You can define filters based on the sender or subject. For example, say each day your client The Red Company sends you an email that you must respond to quickly, and a company called Business News sends you an email newsletter that you're in no rush to read. You can tell your email program to put all messages from Jim@theredcompany.co.uk into a folder called 'Red Company', and all messages from news@business-news.co.uk into your Reading folder. Then you can easily see at a glance when you have a message from the Red Company you need to deal with, and you can ignore the new message in the Reading folder for now.

### Using multiple email addresses

Why not use a different email address for different types of email? Create one specifically for business, one for personal, one for all your newsletters, and one for less important things. It's also advisable to create one you use where you think that you might get spammed – for example, when you sign up for product information on a website.

Using different email addresses may sound complicated but it helps with the sorting process. You can set your mail system to pick up multiple accounts and then check the important ones regularly and the less important ones, less often. For example, non-essential newsletters can go to one email address that you check now and again, and work-related emails can go to your main account that you check regularly.

It's easy to set up a new mail address in Hotmail, Yahoo, Gmail, or your email provider. You can then forward most of these email accounts on to one preferred email account.

You can also 'Send mail as' so you can reply in, say, your Gmail account but as if you're in your Hotmail account. This makes it easy to handle various accounts from one email application such as Outlook or Thunderbird.

## Using templates

Take a look at the types of emails you send out on a regular basis and think about using a template to speed up your response. You can make a template for each different type of email that you can use over and over again, rather than creating it from new each time. This saves you time and effort.

You can create your template in a word processing programme, and then just cut and paste the text into your mail system as needed.

# Following email etiquette

Don't just consider your own time management when dealing with emails – spare a thought for the recipient too. Follow the pointers below to make sure that you don't frustrate, bore, or offend with your emails.

✔ **Auto responder:** If necessary, set an auto responder so that people who email you can automatically be notified that you've received their emails and you'll get back to them within a specified time.

✔ **Addressees:** Only send an email to the person who actually needs to read it. Don't copy in everyone unless you need to: use the cc and bcc fields appropriately. Use the cc field to copy in someone who may want to read the email for information, and the bcc field when you send an email out to a number of users and you don't want to reveal the email addresses to all recipients.

✔ **Capitals:** Don't use capitals – this is seen as SHOUTING in the online world.

✔ **Content:** Keep emails short and precise, and watch your spelling, punctuation, and grammar. Avoid the use of jargon or abbreviations unless you know that the reader is familiar with the topic. Make sure that your meaning is clear, and include the original email when you reply to make it easier

to follow the thread of a discussion. Remove any unnecessary previous messages and ensure that the Subject field contains something relevant. Finally, re-read your email before you hit Send.

✔ **Delivery:** Emails aren't 100 per cent guaranteed to reach their recipients, especially with spam filters getting more and more efficient/aggressive/selective. You can't be sure that your email has been delivered and there can also be a time delay in pressing Send and it turning up in the recipient's inbox. If it's urgent, pick up the phone.

You can also look into getting a tool like Spam Assassin, (www.spamassassin.apache.org) which checks your email for the key flags that it identifies as spam and provides a rating. A spam filter is useful if you send out a regular newsletter or mailing to your contact list and is often built into newsletter and email distribution tools.

✔ **Hoaxes/chain letters:** *Never* forward hoaxes or chain letters. They waste everyone's time. Bill Gates is *not* going to give you money for forwarding that email as part of Microsoft research. And virus warning messages are probably hoaxes or contain viruses themselves. (Make sure

*(continued)*

that you have virus protection installed on your computer)

✔ **Length:** Don't waffle on in an email – keep to the point. Longer emails are more difficult to read.

✔ **Request Read Receipt:** If you want to know that an email has been received, set the Receipt requested option. But you may not automatically get a receipt if the recipient chooses not to send confirmation of reading. Don't set this as the default – it's not necessary.

Use the template as the basis for your email, but make sure that you personalise the message in some way. You don't want to send a stilted and impersonal email that makes your use of a template obvious to the recipient.

## Clearing the clutter

Although the Internet is great for finding information, if you're anything like me, you just love signing up for things – special offers, bulletins, newsletters, forums, and so on. As a result, you end up on more and more mailing lists, and receiving more and more emails, which take up more and more of your time to wade through.

Make sure that every few months you go through your inbox or reading and newsletter folders and unsubscribe from communications you haven't read or that are no longer useful.

There's no point in cluttering up your inbox with things that you're never going to get round to reading. If you haven't made time to read the communication in the week it arrives, the chances are you won't get round to looking at it or, if you do, then the information is already out of date. And if you need to find the information the email contains, you can probably access it on the original website or find it through a search engine.

## Avoiding spam

Unfortunately, you can't avoid receiving any spam at all, but you do have a few ways of dealing with it once you start receiving it.

The best way to avoid spam is to be selective about who you give your email address to. For example, posting your email address on a website guarantees that automated email grabbers can pick up your address, and then send spam to it. Publishing your address on various directories or public listings also increases the risk of receiving more and more spam.

Thankfully most email providers have a junk and spam filter option that automatically sends email it identifies as potential spam into a separate folder or just deletes it. You can usually opt to do the same with emails that come from an address you don't recognise.

You can also find spam filters that plug into your mailbox and filter out the spam for you. Most of these filters need initial 'training' so they can identify what is spam and you need to check the spam folder regularly to make sure that valid emails aren't being marked as spam.

Here are a few of these spam filters:

- ✔ CA Anti-spam (www.ca-store.co.uk, costs about £40).
- ✔ Mailwasher (www.firetrust.com, costs about £20).
- ✔ McAfee Spam Killer (www.spamkiller.com, costs about £20).
- ✔ Norton AntiSpam (www.norton.com costs about £40 a year).
- ✔ Spam Eater (www.spameater.com, costs about £9 a year).

Protect yourself from viruses, which are invariably passed in spam messages by installing good virus protection such as McAfee, Norton, CA AntiVirus, or AVG Anti-Virus (free).

You can check reviews of the latest spam and virus applications on www.zdnet.com.

# Dealing with an Email Backlog

You probably dread coming back from holiday to hundreds if not thousands of emails in your inbox. Your heart sinks at the prospect of spending hours doing little else but dealing with all those emails. Fear not – here are a few ideas to help you minimise and deal with the backlog.

## Preparing before time out

Before you take any time away from work, cancel any email notifications you receive, such as messages from email groups. You can do this for all Yahoo! groups and most online discussion/networking groups. This reduces the volume coming through in the first place so you have fewer messages to deal with.

If you can, set the auto responder on your mail system to automatically send an email telling the sender you're away from the office until a certain date and won't be responding to any emails until your return. If it's urgent, give an alternative contact.

## Handling the deluge when you return

To start with, set aside an hour to go through your inbox. Yes, I know that it's probably going to take much longer than that but at least you make a start.

Don't respond to any new emails until you've cleared what's already in your inbox.

You can tackle the backlog by performing a number of scans:

1. **First scan: Go through quickly and eliminate the spam and any email you know that you don't need to read.**

   Don't read or respond to any emails on this scan. Use the Sort function to sort your email by sender or subject, which makes it easier to delete the junk.

   You don't have time to read everything so delete anything that doesn't require your attention or have information you absolutely *must* have. Don't save it 'just in case'.

2. **Second scan: Pick out all the priority emails you need to respond to first.**

   Place these urgent emails in a separate 'Action' folder. Then set aside time in your diary to respond to your 'Action' emails – do this in that first hour as you should still have a reasonable chunk of the first hour left; if not, set aside more time later in the day.

3. **Third scan: If your filters haven't already sorted out reading emails, now is the time to place them all in the appropriate folder(s).**

   Depending on the volume of emails, you should be able to complete these first two scans in the first hour. Do the third scan too if you still have time; otherwise leave this stage until the next time you're scheduled to work on your email.

4. **Fourth scan: Deal with any remaining emails.**

   Less urgent action emails can now be dealt with. What's left? If it's not action or reading – it's probably not urgent so can be deleted.

Only after you've safely dealt with the backlog that came in while you were away can you apply the same process to the new emails that have come in.

Another method you can use to process your bulging inbox is to create a 'Backlog' folder. Copy all the emails currently in the inbox into this folder. Deal with your inbox in the usual way from now on, and set aside a few minutes each day, or a half an hour a couple of times a week, to deal with the backlog using the scanning method. This way you won't get bogged down with mass of emails in your inbox: you can deal with the new emails and then handle the backlog separately.

# Chapter 9

# Handling Phone Calls

. . . . . . . . . . . . . . . . . . . . . . . . . . . . . . . . . . . . . . . . . . . . .

### In This Chapter

▶ Making the most of time-saving phone features

▶ Preparing for smooth, effective calls

▶ Dealing with outgoing and incoming calls efficiently

▶ Diverting, filtering, and avoiding calls

. . . . . . . . . . . . . . . . . . . . . . . . . . . . . . . . . . . . . . . . . . . . .

*T*he phone can be a great communication tool when it's used effectively. It can also be a great time waster – a distraction that drives you to distraction. In the interest of time management, in this chapter I provide heaps of helpful hints on how to get the best out of your phone. Not only do I address how to successfully manage your time around incoming calls, but I also show you that putting off or rejecting calls sometimes is perfectly okay. In addition, I look at types of phones . . . all with the goal of saving you time in your daily life.

## Getting Organised

This section walks you through some basic preparation that helps you save precious moments when dealing with phone calls.

### Choosing your phone

You have three choices when selecting a phone:

✔ **Cordless phone:** These are a great investment. You're no longer limited, by a length of cord, to the amount of area around which you can pace while you're on the phone.

They give you the freedom to move around the office or home and even wander outdoors if you want to chat and drink your coffee while sitting out in the sunshine.

✔ **Mobile:** A mobile phone gives you complete flexibility – allowing you to keep in touch anytime, anywhere. Most mobiles come with a range of useful features, such as calendars, alarm clocks, and contact systems that can help you be organised and time-efficient. Flick to Chapter 18 for more on mobiles and their personal organiser tools.

✔ **Plug-in phone:** Buy one with an inbuilt speakerphone so you can work with your hands free. You're limited by the length of the cable but not limited by the strength of the signal or the battery running out just at that critical moment.

Cordless and mobile phones need power in order to function. If you have a power failure your cordless phone won't work. Make sure that you have an old analogue phone to plug in the socket in case of emergency or so you can carry on working.

Table 9-1 gives you an idea of helpful features to look for when selecting a phone.

| Table 9-1 | Useful Phone Features | |
|---|---|---|
| *Feature* | *Function* | *Time-saving Use* |
| **Answer machine** | Record a message. | Avoid missing calls or filter calls when busy (see the later section 'Using an answer machine'). |
| **Caller ID** | Identify incoming callers (network dependent). | Screen your calls so you only speak to people you want to. |
| **Handsfree speakerphone** | Project the call out of a speaker so that you don't need to hold the handset. | Free up your hands to do other tasks as you chat; allow other people to join in with the call. |
| **Headphone jack** | Plug in a headset | Talk hands-free and avoid getting a crick in your neck from tucking the phone under your chin. |

| Feature | Function | Time-saving Use |
|---------|----------|-----------------|
| **Phonebook** | Store up to 200 numbers. | Save time finding and dialling numbers. |
| **Redial** | Automatically redial the last number called. | Avoid keying in the number again if you don't get through first time. |
| **Ring tones** | Assign different ring tones for groups of contacts – family, friends, business, clients, and the like. | Recognise callers and decide whether to answer. |
| **Speed dial** | Programme in contacts and dial with one touch of a button. | Save keying frequently used numbers. |
| Store numbers | Save the last 5–10 numbers called. | Redial quickly. |

If you use your speakerphone function, let the caller know and be aware that your call can be overheard by those around you. Don't use the speakerphone for phone calls involving private matters. And don't irritate fellow colleagues by constantly forcing them to listen to your phone conversations (that goes for using a mobile in public as well – yes, we know that you're on the train and we really don't need to hear your discussion about what you're having for dinner . . .).

Also remember the handy features that your phone provider supplies:

✔ **Identifying your last caller:** Dial 1471 and you can find out the last number that rang you (very useful if you missed a call). You can also dial 3 when using this option, to automatically redial the number that last rang you, but your phone provider will probably charge you a hefty premium for this shortcut. Better to jot down the number and redial it yourself!

✔ **Withholding your number:** Dial 141 if you don't want the person you're dialling to know your phone number or that it's you calling. If the person isn't there, he won't know that he's missed your call and you're still in control of when you phone him again.

✔ **Using the ring-back facility:** Your phone provider may also offer a ring-back service. Rather than waste time redialling someone over and over when his line is engaged, you can enter a code and your phone provider rings you back when the line is clear, using a special ringtone so you can differentiate the ring-back call from an ordinary incoming call. All you do is pick up the phone, and your phone provider connects you and starts ringing the other person.

## Managing contacts and numbers

Keep your contact system up to date, whether you have a paper-based address book or index card system, or hold addresses electronically on your computer. Make notes on calls and include them in your contact system. It's useful to know when you last spoke to someone and you can use your calendar to keep track of when to follow-up.

Make sure that you keep important numbers handy when you're likely to need them most. If you're going to a meeting, take a note of the person's number *and* the number for the venue, in case you get lost or delayed and need to contact them.

Save time searching for and dialling numbers by entering the numbers that you call regularly into your phone, especially your mobile. Most handsets on both mobiles and landlines have the ability to store dozens of numbers.

## Preparing for calls

If you've got a number of calls to make, or you're expecting a lengthy call, make yourself comfortable. Grab a glass of water, take a few deep breaths to clear your head, and have any relevant files or information to hand.

Always have pen and paper to hand. It's inevitable that at some point you'll need to write something down and it saves scrabbling round for something to write with and something to write on, or having to leave the caller hanging on while you search round for the necessary tools.

If you work from home, consider having two lines for personal and business. That way, when a business call comes through, you can answer the phone in a professional manner. And having two lines ensures that you can take/make calls when necessary. For example, you can call your client without waiting for your teenage daughter to finish her lengthy discourse on the latest gossip or fashion must-have.

# Making Calls

This section contains a wealth of useful time-saving hints to consider *before* picking up that phone and punching out that number.

Making a phone call can be a sensible way to reach a conclusion, resolve a discussion, stop email ping-pong, or prevent the need for a lengthy and time-consuming meeting.

## Scheduling your calls

Take control of the phone. Set aside a block of time to make several calls together. You can then get through them far more efficiently. Better to get into phone mode and make a number of calls rather than hop from one type of task to another throughout the day.

Make a list of all the phone calls you need to make, along with the relevant numbers, and then you can work through them quickly. If one person isn't available or his voicemail is on – move on to the next one. Work quickly through the list until you reach the end. If you need to go back, schedule the time in for later or add them to the next day's calls.

If you remember a call you have to make while you're working on something else – add it to your list. Don't break the flow by picking up the phone there and then.

## Getting ready for your call

To ensure that you get the best from your phone call, and complete it quickly, prepare before you dial the number. Think about your reason for the call and what you hope to achieve from the conversation. Organise yourself – have the number ready as well as any information you need.

If you don't like making calls or feel uncomfortable on the phone, preparation is key. By considering which questions, reactions, or issues may come up in advance, you can ready yourself to deal with the situation calmly and effectively. If you're prepared you feel much more comfortable about making the call. Be prepared for the answer machine (see the later section 'Leaving Messages').

Before you dial, note down the basic structure for your call in bullet form. Your list enables you to stay on track, the calls flow better, you can cover everything you need to talk about, and you won't forget something important or go blank as soon as the person you're calling picks up the phone. The more you use a structured approach the less you need it and your conversation won't sound too stilted.

You can even write a script for some elements of the conversation. 'What!?' I hear you cry. 'A scripted call can sound terrible. The person is obviously reading word for word, he hardly pauses for breath, and he won't waiver from his spiel if you attempt to interrupt him.'

But to ensure that business calls run smoothly, scripts can be a good idea – and not just for telephone sales people. Your script doesn't have to be rigid, it can give you more confidence as you talk, and it can save time when you regularly make the same sort of calls.

Here's an example of how you may plan your conversation:

1. **Introduce yourself:** 'Hello, this is . . . calling from . . .'

2. **Ask if this is a good time to talk:** 'Are you busy? I just need five minutes of your time.'

3. **State the reason for your call:** 'I'm calling about . . .' 'I'd just like to discuss . . .'

4. **Discuss your key points:** Keep to the point and don't waffle.

5. **Agree any follow-up:** Decide details for any further call, email, or meeting.

6. **Sign off:** Say goodbye, tick the call off your list, and move on with your day. Job done.

# Finding a good time to call

Ideally, you want to call someone when he's available to focus on your call, so that you can get through your business quickly and effectively.

The best time to call someone varies greatly depending on the individual and his work routine. If you know the person well or call him regularly you have a better idea of when you're most likely to catch him in and avoid playing telephone tag.

Bear in mind the following when you're calling people:

✔ At the beginning of the day, and especially Monday mornings, people have just arrived at work and they're sorting out their day and answering emails. This can be a good time to catch them in their office.

✔ At lunchtime you know that people are less likely to be in meetings but more likely to be away from their desk.

✔ At the end of the day, people are keen to get home, especially on a Friday or before they go on holiday, so this can be a good time if you want to keep the call short. Don't call when you know someone's likely to be trying to leave. Call at 4 p.m. rather than 5 p.m.

✔ Contact people who are out and about for most of the day, such as tradespeople, before they leave for work or towards the end of the day – they often have a mobile number for this reason.

Sometimes no time is a good time but you won't know that until you actually make the call. The person may be busy, in a meeting, in the middle of lunch, dinner, getting ready to go home, going out, in the middle of a family crisis, or any other kind of situation.

It makes sense to just ask when the person answers the phone, 'Is this a good time to talk?', or 'Are you free for a few minutes? (but do mean a few minutes). My sister is often busy with family-related activities, so I always ask.

If the person isn't available or is busy and you get through to a secretary or receptionist, ask when would be a convenient time to call, or arrange a specific time when you can talk rather than just saying you'll call back. This saves calling again at some random time and still finding them busy.

## Keeping calls short and sweet

Try to keep calls to five minutes. However, if you know it's going to be a lengthy call, set aside a specific time to talk. That way you're more in control of your time.

Some people like to just talk and talk. Let them know how much time you have available and set a time limit on both yourself and them. Have a way of ending the call on time. To wind up the call, you can say:

✔ 'Just before we finish . . .'

✔ 'We've got five minutes left . . .'

✔ 'I'm expecting another call shortly . . .'

✔ 'I'd like to continue this conversation; can we arrange a time to speak further on . . .?'

Keep an alarm clock or timer by the phone. Set the alarm to ring discretely every hour or start the stopwatch function. If a call drags on, you have an alert to bring you back on track. Some phone displays show the duration of the call.

## Leaving messages

Be prepared for the answer machine to kick-in when you phone someone. Decide before the call if you're going to leave a message or call him back later. If you don't want to leave a message, just hang up if he doesn't answer within a reasonable number of rings.

If you're happy to leave a message, bear in mind the following pointers:

✔ Plan what to say ahead of time. You're less likely to leave a garbled message. You know the sort: 'Umm, err, it's . . ., I err . . .'

✔ Ever wondered why people don't call you back? It may be because they couldn't understand your message. Speak slowly and clearly. Because you can never guarantee the quality of the line (or the writing speed of the listener), it helps if you repeat key information slowly – especially the number.

✔ At the very least, leave your name, the date and time of your call, your number, the reason for the call, and when would be a good time for them to call you or if you'll call them.

✔ If you need them to call within a specific time, say so:

- 'I'll be in the office from . . . until . . .'
- 'Please call me back today.'
- 'If you can call me by the end of the week . . .'

✔ If you've said that you'll call back at a particular time on a certain day, add an entry in your calendar or diary to remind you and include the number.

✔ If you leave a clear, succinct message for someone, you can leave the ball in his court and wait for him to call you. But make a note if you need to follow up at some point if you haven't heard back from him.

# Receiving Calls

In this section I give you the low-down on the best ways to handle incoming calls so you stay productive, efficient, and blissfully stress-free.

You don't have to answer the phone just because it's ringing. If you know you don't want to be disturbed and that you're going to defer the call anyway, then just don't answer the phone in the first place. You *can* resist!

## Maximising your time

With a little know-how, you can make the best of your time before, during, and after the call:

✔ While waiting for an incoming call, do some of your low priority tasks, write a few notes, catch up on some filing, or organise your calendar.

✔ A ringing phone distracts you from what you're working on. By the time you hang up, you've forgotten what you were doing before you were interrupted. 'Now, where was I . . .? Oh yes . . .' When the phone rings, have pen and paper to hand. Make a note of what you're working on so that you can quickly go back to it when you finish the call.

✔ If you're put on hold during the call, put the call on speakerphone and do something else while you're waiting. Alternatively, you can just leave a message and call back later, or ask the caller to ring you again.

## Smooth operators' phone etiquette

A little phone etiquette goes a long way to ensuring a smooth phone call.

✔ Smile when you answer the phone: it makes a difference. Nothing is worse than hearing a bored, miserable voice on the end of the phone and it doesn't give a good impression.

✔ Moderate your tone of voice and language to that of the caller. If it's a business call be professional and avoid being too familiar or casual unless it's someone you know well.

✔ Whenever you answer the phone, particularly at work, at the very least give your name and/or the company or department, so that people know they've reached the right number.

✔ Don't leave a caller hanging on if you need to go and speak to someone else or find some information. If you need to put him on hold, ask first and let him know how long you'll be, or offer to call him back.

✔ If a caller becomes emotional or angry, speak in a calm manner and don't raise your voice or use inflammatory language – it only makes the situation worse. If he's being unreasonable or just getting more irate, it may be best to end the call and offer to call him back or ask him to call later. It's rarely a good idea just to hang up, however rude someone becomes. It just winds him up even more.

✔ If you need to take a message, note down the name, number, and reason for the call. Ask him to spell a name or address if you're not clear and repeat the number to make sure that you have it correctly.

✔ Close off the call by summarising the key points you've discussed and agreeing on any next steps. Who needs to do what? When do you next need to speak to this person? Agree this during the call so there's no margin for error or misunderstanding, and if necessary confirm in writing or email. Getting things straight at this point saves you wasting time after the call trying to sort out what's what.

Sometimes recording your calls can be useful so that you can refer back to them later or take notes. Many answer machines enable you to record the call. However, make sure that you let the caller know that you're recording the call and get his agreement.

If several of you are working in the same office, can you take it in turns to answer the phone? Each of you would then have a block of time to work in with one less distraction.

## Dealing with nuisance calls

The best ways to protect yourself from time-consuming irritating, unwanted calls are to go ex-directory, opt out of the electoral role listing, and be very particular about who you give your number to.

You can deal with specific problem calls in some of the following ways:

✔ **Cold calls:** You can avoid (but not totally eliminate) unwanted, annoying sales call by registering with the Telephone Preference Service (see the sidebar 'Thwarting sales callers'). The later section 'I'd love to talk to you, but . . .' contains more helpful advice for deflecting sales calls.

✔ **Offensive or harassing calls:** These are unpleasant and upsetting. Don't respond – just hang up or leave the phone off the hook. Report such calls to the police.

✔ **Scam calls:** If you get an automated message saying you've won a prize (usually a holiday or product) ignore it. These are just phone scams – they leave a premium rate number to call back and you end up spending several pounds to listen to further automated messages.

✔ **Silent calls:** These are usually the result of automated dialling systems – just hang up.

## *'I'd love to talk to you, but . . .'*

If you're lucky, the first thing your caller asks when you pick up the phone is whether you're okay to talk. But most people seem to see you answering the phone as an invitation to talk, and they just launch straight into the conversation. So don't feel guilty if you need to interrupt and effectively say 'Go away' to the caller.

Here's the situation: it's teatime and the phone rings. You don't have Caller ID, so you're not sure who's calling and whether you want to talk to the person. It may be that call from the bank you've been waiting for all week, but on the other hand, it may be yet another sales call interrupting your dinner. Taking a deep breath, you answer . . . and are greeted by the dulcet tones of a conservatory salesman flogging a once-in-a-lifetime-simply-amazing-not-to-be-missed special offer.

Grrr! How do you deflect the eager advances of this salesman and get off the phone and back to your bangers and mash? If you've got a few minutes and are feeling brave or naughty, you can play him at his own game.

✔ Put the phone down and wander off and do something else – just leave him hanging on and he'll soon hang up.

✔ Start relating your latest tale of woe (can be totally made up) – you're so glad he called, you just needed someone to talk to . . .

Now here's a slightly different situation, where you don't want to say 'Go away', but rather 'Come back later'.

The phone rings when you're already busy with something. You know that your colleague Bob said that he'd call this morning to discuss a project you're working on. You answer the phone and it's Bob. You want to talk to him, but not right now.

Your aim is to shift this phone call to a later, more convenient time. Depending on when you want to chat to Bob, try the following:

    ✔ 'I'm sorry, I'm just on my way out.'

    ✔ 'My other phone is ringing . . .'

    ✔ 'I'm expecting a call.'

    ✔ 'I'm in a meeting.'

Then follow up with one of these phrases:

    ✔ 'Can I call you back in a few minutes?'

    ✔ 'When can I call you back?'

    ✔ 'Can you call me in an hour/later this afternoon/ tomorrow?'

If you're deferring the call, agree a specific date and time for the person to call back or for you to call him. Add it to your calendar or schedule. Nothing is worse than waiting for a promised phone call that never materialises.

## Using an answer machine

An answer phone or voicemail is essential to capture calls when you're unavailable. You can also use it to filter your calls – leaving you free to get on with your work and only take important calls.

---

## Thwarting sales callers

Register with the Telephone Preference Service (TPS) to avoid unwanted sales and marketing calls. Companies have a legal obligation *not* to call consumers who have registered with the TPS.

Register online at www.tps online.org.uk/tps. After about a month a lot of those cold sales calls and silent calls stop. If you do get unsolicited sales calls, ask how they got your number and ask to be taken off their list. Mention that you're registered with TPS and will report them if they call again. That should be enough to stop any further calls.

Remember that if you already have a relationship with a company they may still call you, unless you specifically request not to be contacted.

As well as using the answer phone outside working hours, how about setting aside a block of time in the day when you can focus solely on work without the distraction of calls? Whether it's an hour or two, or a whole afternoon, let all calls go through to your answer machine or voicemail.

Some general tips for getting the best out of your answer machine include:

- ✔ On your incoming answer machine message, leave a personal message, so the caller knows he's got through to the right number. It's annoying to hear the standard default message and not know if it's the right person. Update your message regularly and listen back to it to make sure that it sounds smooth and that you've not included any 'ums and 'errs'. Re-record it until it sounds right.

- ✔ If appropriate, give an alternate contact number, such as a mobile.

- ✔ Set aside time to listen to the messages and call people back as soon as you can, especially if it relates to something important. Missed or delayed calls can mean missed opportunities.

- ✔ Consider using an answering service, particularly for business. Your callers get to talk to a real person and are more likely to leave a message. Answer machines can put people off, so you may miss callers without realising it.

- ✔ Never say you're out or away on holiday on a message – that's just asking for trouble, especially if someone knows your address. Just say you're busy or unavailable.

## *Switching off completely*

Yes, I know that's a scary thought but you really *don't* need to be contactable 24 hours a day, 7 days a week – unless of course you're a doctor on call, have a sick or elderly relative, or it's a critical part of your work (IT support for the Bank of England), or you've children.

If you want some undisturbed time then switch the phone off (or unplug it). Even if it's just for a couple of hours – you can get on with work with one less interruption.

If you're in a meeting switch off your phone – it's rude to interrupt your conversation in order to answer the phone. If you're expecting an important call (and it really does need to be more important than the person or people in front of you) or it's relevant to the discussion, then let your colleagues know you're expecting a call.

# Chapter 10

# Dealing with Distractions and Interruptions

. . . . . . . . . . . . . . . . . . . . . . . . . . . . . . . . . . . . . . . . . . . . .

## *In This Chapter*

▶ Thinking about what distracts you

▶ Fielding people and phone calls

▶ Using distractions to good effect

. . . . . . . . . . . . . . . . . . . . . . . . . . . . . . . . . . . . . . . . . . . . .

*G*oing through a day without being distracted or interrupted by one thing or another is almost impossible.
Distractions and interruptions are just symptoms of a busy
life and the constant demands on your time, whether you're in
the office or at home.

A *distraction* takes your attention away from the task in front of
you to focus on something else, often something more
interesting!

An *interruption* is when an external force, such as the phone
ringing or a person walking into your office and asking a
question, breaks your attention.

As a human being, you're naturally curious and that means
you have a tendency to switch from one task to another as
something new catches your interest. In everyday life you can
be distracted from something uninteresting or taxing, towards
something more interesting and less boring or difficult.

Sometimes you'd be so much more effective in managing your
time if you didn't get constantly interrupted. This chapter helps
you keep distractions and interruptions to a minimum so that
you can better manage your time.

# Identifying the Culprits

Think about the things that distract or interrupt you during your day and eat away at your time. These may include:

- ✔ Chat
- ✔ Email
- ✔ Internet
- ✔ Meetings
- ✔ People
- ✔ Phone calls
- ✔ Television

Consider how much of your time you spend on unimportant emails, phone calls, interruptions, and low priority tasks. Make a note of the typical interruptions and distractions that occur during a normal working day, using the form shown in Table 10-1.

| Table 10-1 | Identifying Interruptions |
|---|---|
| Date: | |
| Time: | |
| Who/What (phone, email, person, yourself): | |
| Duration: | |
| Reason: | |

Take a look at the causes of your interruptions and distractions. Identify steps you can take to reduce these distractions and take control of your time – I show you how in this chapter.

You need to have some flexibility to be able to deal with interruptions – if interruptions are an everyday occurrence or part of your job you need to make allowances for them. Give yourself a little extra time in your day. Priorities can change at short notice, so you need to be flexible and reassess things throughout the day.

Interruptions can provide an ideal excuse not to do the work you're actually focusing on – an excuse to procrastinate (see Chapter 2). If a friend calls up and suggests meeting for a coffee, saying 'yes' is very easy when you're working on your accounts but is the last thing you need to do in the scope of time management!

When you get distracted or interrupted, ask yourself the question: 'Is this the best use of my time right now?'

Are you going to succumb to the distraction or interruption, or get back to the task in hand? How is the distraction going to impact on your tasks and goals for the day if you allow it to continue? Focus on what you really need to do.

If you start to organise your time efficiently and put systems in place, you'll be able to deal with interruptions and disruptions more effectively – avoiding some altogether, and being better able to deal with the ones that do occur.

# Getting Hung Up on Phone Calls

You're just settling into preparing your notes for an important presentation when . . . brrring-brrring! The phone rings and you completely lose your concentration, and waste time trying to regroup.

If you have work to do and need some undisturbed time, use the answering machine to screen your calls or switch the phone through to a colleague.

If you have to, switch the phone off or unplug it completely, so that you won't be distracted by it ringing even before the answering machine kicks in or it diverts. Just remember to switch it back on when you've finished!

If you're interrupted by a phone call, and it's obvious that the call is going to take longer than a couple of minutes, arrange with the caller to talk later in the day, or week, rather than rushing the call or feeling pressured because you want to get back to the task in hand. Chapter 9 gives lots more information about handling phone calls.

# Fielding the Demands of Other People

How many times have you heard the question 'Have you got a minute?' What that question actually means is 'I've got a problem or a question, can you help me?'

You know that it's not going to be 'a minute' and that if you say 'Yes', not only have you allowed the interruption to continue but you may well end up with another task to do as a result.

If you get interrupted and it's not convenient – say so! If you're busy, tell the person that you can get back to them later in the day or tomorrow when you have more time. If she presses you, put a time limit on the interruption. Make sure that 'two minutes' really is two minutes. (You can find loads more about setting your boundaries in Chapter 5.)

Stand up to talk – it's more difficult to have a long chat if both of you are standing.

## Making appointments

Try not to let people interrupt you as a matter of course. If someone needs a chunk of your time, rather than doing so on the spur of the moment when you may be busy working on something else, she needs to schedule some time with you. Once people get used to this approach, you'll be interrupted less often.

Having to make an appointment has the added benefit of making people think about what they want to discuss with you – and perhaps come up with their own solution before asking you.

If you work with staff, let them know when you're available and when you don't want to be interrupted. Let your PA or secretary handle as many of the interruptions as possible and book appointments.

## *Finding some quiet space*

To avoid being interrupted at your desk while you're at work, book a meeting room or use an empty office for a couple of hours and shut yourself away. If you have your own office, shut the door and get people used to the fact that if your door is shut you don't want to be disturbed.

 Use a 'Do Not Disturb' sign on your door. Alternate it with an 'Available' sign, so people know when they can talk to you. This works in your home office too.

If your company allows flexible working, work from home on important projects. You get less interruption from people just 'dropping by' your desk – but you still need to resist the lure of the television/housework/lie-in, and other attractions!

# *Utter Clutter: Keeping Your Environment Distraction-Free*

Look around at your office space and your physical environment in general. Are you working in a noisy or cluttered space? Do people walk past your desk and disturb you? Do piles of paper, files, and office toys distract you? The following tips can help you to concentrate and improve your time management:

✔ Move your desk if you can, so that people walking past don't distract you.

✔ Keep your paperwork organised so that you're not distracted or wasting time trying to find something. Use the walls, whiteboards, and pinboards to keep things in view without unnecessary mess and clutter.

✔ Put away or tidy up your paperwork at the end of the day so that you're not distracted when you start work in the morning. (Check out Chapter 7 for more on dealing with paperwork.)

✔ When you work from home, keep distractions such as watching television or washing the dishes to a minimum. Schedule them into your day so that they become intentions rather than distractions.

# Internet Interruptions

You probably spend a lot of time on the Internet, whether for business or for social reasons. You know the scene – you click on a link and then another, and then suddenly something you read leads you off in a totally different direction.

The large number of online networking and blogging sites such as Facebook and YouTube can be a huge source of distraction.

Perhaps you'd like to spend less time online, or simply be more organised in the way that you surf. Manage your time online in the same way that you manage any other area of your business or social life.

## Keep tabs on online networking

Are you a fiend for networking and blogging sites? Losing track of time is easy when you're absorbed like this, but be careful that you don't lose all sense of self-discipline.

Think about why you use online networking. Set yourself goals for your time online, such as posting a set number of blogs, and connecting with a certain number of new members, per week. How much do you contribute to the groups and networks you're a member of? Some you may need to check every day; some only need to be checked once or twice a week.

Limit yourself to 15–30 minutes per day to post, read, and comment on blogs, to connect with people, and for reading. Allocate set times to do any regular group postings, such as once a week or, if postings are key to your business, once a day.

## Message alert settings

You can change how often you're alerted that a message has been posted or updated, to a level appropriate for each of your online groups or networks as part of your time management goals. For example, in Yahoo your options include:

✔ **Daily:** You're notified once a day of new messages or posts.

✔ **Digest:** You receive one email with all the day's messages, or a summary.

✔ **Immediate:** You receive an instant email for every new message or post.

✔ **None:** You only receive messages from the Administrator.

For the networks you're more active on, set the notification to Immediate, which can make it easier to keep track of discussions or for topics to which you've contributed or need to know about. This is particularly useful if they relate to your business or area of expertise. For others set the notification to Daily, Digest, or None.

Check the list of groups and networks you're a regular member of and leave those you no longer use or that have become less active.

Create an email folder for each network so that you can easily see what's new and then you can quickly scan through the messages. Chapter 8 offers more time-saving tips about email.

## Surfing into the blue yonder

Once you start surfing the Internet there's no limit to where you can go or where you may end up, which can really waste your time.

Search engines such as Google can lead you down all sorts of interesting but perhaps irrelevant pathways and off at a tangent. Given the nature of human curiosity, you usually end up several sites away from where you originally intended and probably on a completely different topic from when you set out.

If you go on to the Internet for a specific reason, make sure that you stick to the task in hand and set yourself a time limit.

If you find yourself popping online to check out the latest gadget, gizmo, online bargain, or celebrity gossip, follow these tips:

✔ Ask yourself if you should really be doing this in work time (if you are).

✔ Tell your partner, family member, or housemate to come and kick you off if you've exceeded a certain time. Or you can set a timer.

✔ Download the application RescueTime if you really want to scare yourself into how productive (or not) you are. This program monitors where you spend your time on the computer, such as emailing, surfing, or working. Check out www.rescuetime.com.

Nothing's wrong with taking a break from work to check what's going on in your online network, especially if you work from home and doing so is the equivalent of chatting with colleagues in the office.

However, if you use instant messaging software like AIM, Yahoo, Windows Messenger, or Skype to connect with people, switch it off or change your status when you don't want to be disturbed.

## Keeping to a Time Limit

If you get easily distracted throughout your working day, set yourself a time limit when you're working on a task. You're less likely to go off on a tangent or get distracted if you know that you've only got a fixed amount of time in which to complete the task.

Setting a time limit has the same effect as setting a deadline. It helps to focus the mind, making you more productive with the time available.

If you decide to spend a 'few minutes' checking emails, check them for five minutes only before moving on to something else. Set a time limit and stick to it.

Organise your time and plan out your activities in the day. Set aside specific times to write emails and make phone calls.

Get yourself a kitchen timer and set it to the time you have to complete the task you're working on.

# Motivating Yourself with Rewards

Distractions can often be more pleasurable or easier than the task you're currently focusing on. You can use this fact to your advantage by giving yourself a more pleasant task (or distraction!) as a reward for completing a task. You now have an incentive to get the task done and reach your reward more quickly.

Only allow yourself to be distracted *after* you've completed the task.

Your company may give you a bonus as a reward for achieving your target or completing a project, so why not do this for yourself in a small way?

---

## All work and no play

Elsewhere in this book I mention the need for frequent fun breaks and changes of activity to keep you motivated, focused, and productive. These fun breaks are also necessary when you're at work!

Find ways to make tasks fun:

✔ Shuffle tasks – mix up unappealing tasks with more pleasant ones.

✔ Make your workspace fun and creative.

✔ Use colour and images on your calendar, diary, sticky notes, and folders for different types of tasks.

✔ Do something different each day, such as taking a different route to

work, eating something new for lunch, and using your less domi-nant hand to do things like using the mouse.

✔ Smile and say thank you more often.

✔ Team up with a buddy or col-league when you can so you're not working on your own.

✔ Make a game of work – how many calls can you make, how many files can you clear, how quickly can you complete a task?

By making work fun, you become more focused and less likely to get distracted.

---

From small, simple, inexpensive rewards for daily tasks to larger more expensive rewards for completing a major project on time, make the reward match the amount of effort involved. Your reward may be to:

✔ Make a coffee.

✔ Enjoy a glass of your favourite wine.

✔ Eat chocolate.

✔ Listen to music.

✔ Go for a walk.

✔ Have a teatime treat.

✔ Buy a new book, CD, or DVD.

✔ Go to the cinema.

✔ Spend time with your partner or a close friend.

✔ Go for a meal at your favourite restaurant.

✔ Buy a new outfit.

✔ Book a spa day or massage.

✔ Reserve tickets for the theatre.

✔ Have a day off.

✔ Arrange a weekend away.

✔ Organise a holiday.

Each time you complete a particular task or achieve a milestone, put a £1 coin in a jar. Put in even more when you've done so on time. At the end of the year, or when you've completed the goal, you can treat yourself.

# Chapter 11

# Perfecting the Art of Delegation

*H*owever much you've got to do, at some point you have to admit that you can't do everything yourself. In other chapters I show you ways in which you can organise all your day-to-day tasks more effectively. But as I explain in this chapter, sometimes it's better to let someone else do the work for you.

Delegating is one of the key skills to master so that you can make better use of your time. You only have so many hours in your day, so if you haven't got enough time to get everything done then find someone else to do certain things for you. The more you learn to effectively delegate, the more time you free up to focus on other important tasks.

In Chapter 2 I show you how to work out how much your time is worth. Use this as a guide when looking at when and what you need to delegate. Your workload is limited by the amount of hours you have available – increase the number of hours and you increase your productivity and what you can achieve each day. One hour of your own effort achieves one hour of results. Delegate a task and one hour of effort can achieve several hours of results.

# Letting Go

You may be quite happy to let someone else help you out and do some of your work, or you may have trouble letting go of parts of your workload. Some people find it easier to delegate than others.

Reasons why you don't delegate perhaps include:

- ✔ No one else can do it as well as me. They won't do it right. If you want something done properly, you do it yourself.
- ✔ It takes too long to show someone else how to do it.
- ✔ If someone else does the work for me, I'll lose control of the job.
- ✔ I particularly enjoy this task, even if it's not the best use of my time.
- ✔ If I'm constantly busy I feel important and indispensable.

If you want to get more done, then delegate more – don't try to keep control of everything.

Delegation is good for other people. Your team members benefit as you develop their skills and abilities, motivation, and responsibility. The more you do, the more you improve your leadership and delegation skills. Don't micro-manage people – give them responsibility for their own work.

And don't be put off delegating just because you think that the other person isn't good enough. Give people a chance and don't expect them to get it right first time. It's worth it in the long-run when you gain an extra two hours each week to work on something that needs your undivided attention.

# Asking for Help

You don't need to do everything, although many people feel that they 'should' and don't ask for help when they need it – preferring to flounder on until it's too late or they crumble under the weight of everything they're trying to do.

One of the problems many people face is knowing when to ask for help. No one can cope with everything single-handed, so don't see asking for help as a sign of weakness. You have your own skills and abilities, other people have theirs, so make effective use of both. Stick to what you're good at and let other people do what they're good at.

Here are some signs that you need to ask for help:

✔ You're working long hours and feel you've taken on too much.

✔ You've exhausted your resources dealing with a particular problem.

✔ You're a perfectionist and feel overwhelmed trying to create a perfect solution.

You may see yourself as being reliable, capable, and able to cope with everything that your boss asks you to do or that life has to throw at you. You just get on and do things – keeping yourself busy, moving forward, juggling work, life, children, partners, friends and family. The British approach is to soldier bravely on, not admitting that a helping hand may actually be needed.

Be brave. Put your hand up if you need help – whether that's from friends, family, or a professional.

# Getting Systems in Place

In any given day you perform a number of tasks – making phone calls, sending emails, writing, data entry, meeting clients and customers – whatever is relevant to your work. Are you able to describe to someone else what it is you do? If not then you're not going to be able to delegate that task very easily. You probably don't even think about most of what you do, you just do it automatically, but would someone else know how to do it if he wasn't shown how?

Writing things down not only makes it easier to hand tasks over to someone else but is a good way to check that things are being done efficiently. What documents and checklists do you use to track your progress?

You can document what you do as you go along. As work comes in, think about all the different steps you take to process it and the various references you use. Write it all down. While you want to make life easy for yourself and better manage your time by delegating certain tasks, don't make life more difficult for the person you're delegating to.

For example, if you want someone to do your accounts, then you need to have a system for him to work with to make it easy to hand this task over. Although it does happen, no one's going to be impressed by being handed a carrier bag of receipts at the end of the year. At least put them in a different file or folder for each month and keep *all* your receipts and invoices together.

# Knowing What to Delegate

To be successful and effective at delegating – delegate the right tasks, at the right time, to the right people. Yousave yourself time by being spot on when you delegate a given task so you don't have to go back and re-delegate it.

## Remembering the do's and don'ts

Having established you need help and identified what you need help with, don't just dump all your jobs on to someone else. You can't delegate everything. You're always going to need to keep control of certain tasks yourself.

Do delegate:

- ✔ When you're not the best person for the job.

- ✔ Tasks that someone else can do faster, better, and cheaper than you can.

- ✔ Tasks you don't like doing yourself and that aren't your main skill set.

- ✔ Your routine tasks – freeing you up to do more complex or important tasks.

- ✔ Jobs for which you're overqualified – for example, if you're a highly paid executive why would you spend your time answering the phone rather than doing your job?

✔ Tasks to another department that's better able to handle the job or whose responsibility it is – for example, the human resources department can handle recruitment, and customer services may deal with customer problems and queries.

✔ Any tasks for which you need specialist advice – you may think that you can do it yourself but in the long run you save time and money if you get someone in with the skills to do the job in the first place.

Don't delegate:

✔ Anything that's confidential in nature – for example, keep personnel issues like hiring, firing, and pay-related issues as your responsibility.

✔ Tasks that are critical for you to do yourself.

✔ To someone who clearly isn't able to do the task – you're setting the person and yourself up for failure, which just reinforces the reason you didn't want to delegate in the first place.

## Sharing the burden at work

Don't fall into the trap of feeling you need to do everything at work. Delegating can be a useful way of freeing up more time.

✔ **Accounts:** If you have to do your own accounts and this is something you don't have time for or resist doing, get a bookkeeper or accountant. Paying them for a couple of hours' work, once a month is a far better use of your time. They have the knowledge and experience and can do it faster and do a far better job than you.

✔ **Admin:** Most offices have an admin assistant to carry out routine tasks such as photocopying, printing, filing, data entry, taking calls, booking travel, and making meeting arrangements. Even if you work for yourself why not consider employing an admin assistant for a couple of hours a week? You don't need to have one full time and it would free you up to do other things.

Use *Virtual Assistants* – professionals who work from home for other businesses. They can handle all your admin requirements without the need to be there in person. They have a variety of skills depending on the work you want them to do – call handling, email, invoicing, word processing, spreadsheets, editing, presentations, and research.

✔ **Creative:** You may want to create your own website from scratch but do you really have the time to sit down and learn Frontpage, html code, and all about FTP? Get in a professional. The same applies to graphic design – even though you may be able to knock something up on your word processor with a few clip-art images, it's worth paying a professional.

✔ **Technical:** Don't waste time trying to deal with a technical issue. Pick up the phone and get in an expert – if you have an in-house IT department that's what they're there for.

If you work for yourself, check out Chapter 12, which suggests a list of people you can have in your support team and gives you an idea of the types of work you can delegate.

## Getting help at home

If you want to enjoy your 'down' time more, you have plenty of opportunities to delegate tasks around the home by involving the rest of the family or getting someone in.

✔ **Chores:** Rope in the family to help out with the household chores. Plenty of small jobs can be done in exchange for pocket money or taxi duties. You don't have to do all the washing, ironing, and cooking yourself. Even small children can be given simple tasks to do that saves you having to do them – such as putting their toys away at the end of the day.

✔ **Cleaning:** Paying someone to come in and clean your house once a week for a couple of hours is worth its weight in gold (and so are good cleaners). Think about your hourly rate. How much do you earn, and how much would it cost you to pay someone to do your housework once a week? It frees you up to enjoy your space without feeling that your evenings and weekends need to be taken up with keeping the housework under control. You can keep on top of things more easily if the basics have been dealt with. It's much easier to keep a clean house tidy.

✔ **DIY:** We all know what a great nation of DIYers the Brits are, but how much time does it take to do even a simple thing, like painting a room? First you have the preparation time when you clear the room and wash down the walls; then you have the priming, painting, and woodwork; and finally tidying up and putting everything back. That can easily take up a whole weekend, so why not pay someone to come in and do it for you? He can do a much more professional job, far quicker than you and the cost is well worth the benefit of having a whole weekend to yourself.

Why not pay someone to come and finish up all the odd jobs you've been meaning to get around to for months? Half plastered walls, leaky taps, new plug sockets – a handyman (or woman) can get all these jobs done and out of the way in just a few hours. What you pay to get the work done is worth it for the time, effort, and energy you save, and not having the stress of half-finished jobs lying around.

✔ **Gardening:** Although you may enjoy gardening, you probably don't have too much time – other than at the weekends when you have plenty of other things that you'd like do, one of which is enjoying your garden rather than working on it. Consider paying someone to come in once a week to mow the lawn or once a month for a couple of hours to tidy things up.

Establish routines around the house – laundry gets done on certain days and needs to be in the wash basket or it doesn't get done. Blitz one room a week to keep it under control. Employ the principle of little and often to stop things piling up.

# Understanding How to Delegate

Here are some essential tips for successful delegation.

## Planning in advance

Don't dump stuff on people just because you haven't got round to doing it yourself – that's poor time management and not the way to delegate. If you want someone else to do something for you then let him know about it as soon as possible.

If you give a piece of work to someone, he may need to adjust his priorities, drop a piece of work, or delegate to someone else. Be aware of this when you make a request and don't expect your colleague to drop everything just for you.

## Delegating appropriately

Find the person with the right experience, skills, knowledge, and time to do the task. Ask yourself how does he work, what are his long-term goals, what sort of person is he, and is he the right person for the job? Are you delegating internally to someone else in your team or department, or externally to another professional or outside company?

 When you involve the services of a professional outside of your business (or home) get a variety of prices and recommendations from friends – don't choose purely based on price. Take into account their experience, training, and professional membership.

## Giving instructions

When you give someone work to do, be clear about what it is you want done and when you need it done by – be specific.

- ✔ **What** outcome or results do you expect?
- ✔ **When** do you need it completed? Give a specific date.
- ✔ **How** would you like the work done, and what feedback and updates do you need along the way?
- ✔ **Why** is the work important? What are the benefits or pay-off?

 Put things in writing, so you're both clear on the job description, which means less margin for error and misunderstanding.

Engage the delegated person in the process and let him know what's expected and what he can get out of it – such as recognition, promotion, financial reward, or more responsibility.

Say thank you and show your appreciation to the person helping you. People benefit from verbal encouragement and praise just as much as getting a bonus at the end of the year.

Be patient as you delegate. Whenever you delegate, you need to spend time showing someone what you want. This is time well spent as once you've spent that initial training and learning time, your colleague can then get on with the task the next time. Although you may be able to do it faster yourself, that's only because you know how to do it and you've been doing it for years. You had to learn at some point, so appreciate that others need to go through a learning curve too.

Show, tell, do. Repeat as many times as necessary. Get the delegated person to explain the task back to you, so you know that he's understood. Make sure that you give him all the resources necessary to get the job done – don't hold back.

Finally, make yourself available to answer any questions and provide support where necessary. Don't drop a task on someone and then run away. If he gets it wrong it may be because you haven't explained it clearly.

## Managing the delegated task

As part of your daily planning, follow up on tasks you've delegated. Keep track on the progress of the work without micromanaging the person at every step. Staying involved with the task increases the person's motivation and means you stay in control and can adjust as you go.

Put a reminder in your diary for when you want the work done and give yourself and the other person some leeway. You may want to chase him up a couple of days before you need the work so that he's still got time to get it done, if he hasn't finished it. You've then got time to review the work and give it back to him if there's still more to do or corrections need to be made.

Set certain parameters around the task – identify the other person's boundaries of responsibility and how much authority he has to get the task done. Maintain control and responsibility for the task as a whole. The buck stops with you. The other person needs to know that your support is there if he needs it while being able to get on with the task.

Communication and feedback along the way form an important part in correctly managing a delegated task.

## Achieving the best result

Don't focus on the process but the results. Be open to change. Just because you've always done something in a certain way doesn't mean that it's the only way to do it. If you've delegated a task to someone, let him use his skills and abilities to do it in his own way, as long as the end result is what you want and on time.

Review the task when it's been completed. Don't just accept a piece of work if it's not right. Provide the delegated person with feedback so that he knows he got it right, or what he needs to do to improve next time.

Be patient and don't just give up if the results are less than perfect. Stick with it – delegating really does make a difference to managing your time more effectively.

# Part IV
# Working from Home

"We don't get many visitors since we added
the extension for Geoffrey's home office."

## In this part . . .

1 focus on how you can organise your home environment to create an efficient place to work. Whether you work at home every day or only occasionally, or if you're thinking of setting up an office at home, you'll find helpful ideas in this part. I consider the equipment you need to get started, how to find the best place to work, and your filing, storage, and technology options.

# Chapter 12

# Finding a Time-Efficient Work Style at Home

*M*ore and more people are choosing to work from home these days. It seems like an ideal solution to creating a better work–life balance and although it can be an ideal way of having a flexible working environment, it does have its pitfalls.

Balancing work within the home environment can often be difficult. For example, you may find yourself distracted by household chores, well-meaning friends 'just calling for a chat', or – if you're a parent – the demands of your kids. And you may find it hard to switch off from work, when your in-tray seems to call to you even though you've finished work for the day.

So, to work happily, productively, and time-efficiently at home, you need to create an effective work style. This chapter shows you how . . .

## Identifying Your Needs

Working from home – whether full-time, for a couple of days a week, or for the odd hour (or four) on the occasional evening – requires a work style suited to your needs. Your work style depends on a range of factors such as why you're working from home, how often, and for how long.

Here are some examples of the kinds of people who work from home:

- **People with home-based businesses:** Some self-employed people – such as freelance writers, designers, and consultants – choose to work wholly from their homes. And many entrepreneurs start their new businesses from home, to save money before they need to find separate premises.

- **Salespeople:** They spend much of their day travelling and meeting customers and the rest of the time working from home.

- **Telecommuters:** More companies are now allowing their employees to work from home as *telecommuters* (remote workers), so you may find yourself working fully or partially from home. Most remote workers work a couple of days at home and other days in the main office or at other locations.

All these people have different needs – the demands of their jobs and lives are different, and they work at home at different times and for different durations. To successfully manage their time, they need to recognise and fulfil these needs.

To help you determine your needs, ask yourself the following questions:

- How many hours do you spend working at home?

- Do you run your own business from home or work for someone else?

- Do you have a separate area or room in which you can work?

- Do you need quiet time when you work – all the time or sometimes?

- Do you need space to make things?

- Do you see clients in your home office?

- Do you need to stick to standard office hours or do you have some flexibility?

Keep your answers to these questions in mind as you read the rest of the chapter and settle on a suitable work style that helps you be efficient and effective.

# Creating a Structure for Your Time

When you work from home full-time, your work is always there – it's not a commute across town or a train ride away. The temptation is to work longer hours than you would if working in an office – not only because you have to, but because you want to or because you can. Avoid this pitfall by deciding on (and then sticking to) your working hours. Otherwise, your time management goes out the window.

Take a look at Chapter 4 for general advice on structuring your time.

## Choosing the best-fit structure

When running your own business from home you can usually choose the hours you want to work, but make sure that it's not getting in the way of the rest of your life. Working at weekends can be a good time to catch up on things at the end of the week, or spend some time planning for the week ahead. There's no reason why you need to stick to the 9 to 5 but make sure that on average you're not extending your working hours to a 50–60-hour working week.

If you work as a telecommuter or remote worker, your company may expect you to work a standard 9 to 5 day or have a set amount of work you need to complete within the working week. Some of these tips can still be applied to your working routine. What way of working works best for you? If you can work a few hours each day, you still have time to spend with family and friends. If you like getting an early start – you can finish by 3.30 p.m. each day and have the rest of the afternoon and evening free for other activities and family time.

# Setting your working hours

If you work from home it can be tempting to have a flexible working day that fits in around family and home life. However, this often leads to blurred lines between the two. Although some level of flexibility is fine, creating a structure for your working day makes for more effective time management.

Here are some pointers:

- ✔ **Start work at roughly the same time each day:** You may start early, take a couple of hours break around lunch-time or around the school run and then work in the evening.

- ✔ **Put a limit on break times:** By all means take breaks during the day to have some 'home' life, or time to get chores done, but place a time limit on these.

- ✔ **Set a fixed finish time to your working day:** If you don't, you're likely to end up working late into the evening – just because you still have things to be done and you don't have the natural reminder of your fellow colleagues going home.

- ✔ **Create a structure of core hours in which you work:** Your hours don't need to be rigid but you should build in some consistency.

- ✔ **Plan your time at the beginning of the week:** Perhaps you need to take a half-day during the week for home-based tasks or school commitments – sports day, school play, car servicing, and so on. Book this in and plan your work around it.

Why not plan your working hours across the whole week. How many hours do you work a week on average? Spread them out across six days rather than five, or work four long days and have three days off.

# Planning time out

Think about why you've chosen to work from home instead of working in an office. You should be enjoying your time, not struggling to juggle home life with work life. If you want to have a day or half-day a week when you don't work, then do it. Book it out in your diary in advance.

Take a half-day off once a month to have lunch with your partner or a friend.

Planning time out is essential for happy, productive working. If you start having to work long hours or work at weekends or your family and friends are complaining that they never see you, then you need to look at whether your existing time structuring is really working.

# Drawing a Line Between Work and Play

In Chapter 5, I explain the importance of setting boundaries – for your productivity, your time management and, of course, your sanity. Boundaries can become very blurred when you work from home. The following sections address the two biggest boundary-encroaching culprits.

## Tackling the work creep

You've tidied your desk, shut down your PC, and stepped away from your work space – you've finished work for the day. But if you haven't set firm boundaries between work and home, then that work can creep into your 'me time'.

To draw a clear line between work and home, consider the following:

Set your working hours – including evening and weekends – and keep to them as much as possible.

- ✔ **Close the door on your office.** This creates a clearer boundary between your work space and your home space. If there's no door to close on your work space – for example, your desk is in a corner of the lounge – use a simple folding screen or curtain to close off that area of the room.

- ✔ **Be 'out of the office'.** If your work phone rings during the evening or at the weekend, you don't have to answer it. The same goes for replying to emails. Switch on the answer phone and steer clear of emails.

People shouldn't expect you to be working. If you start getting into the habit of answering the phone or dealing with emails outside of your defined office hours then people start to expect that and keep calling/emailing.

Don't allow yourself to get into the habit of working all hours – late into the evening or at weekends – just because your office is at home, only a few feet away and you can just 'pop in' to check emails.

## (Politely) dealing with family and friends

Although it's one of the benefits of working from home, having family and friends around can also be a distraction. Be mindful of other people around you – if you're at home, they may expect you to be more involved.

Let family and friends know when you're working and when you're not. Try something simple like putting a note on your office door when you're working and don't want to be disturbed. Explain when you can spend time with them, and when you need space, time, or some peace and quiet.

Your family and friends need to know that if you're in your office, you're working. If you get distracted, take a complete break and then get back into work mode. If they call or interrupt you when you're working mention that you're busy and let them know that you'll call them back later (read more about boundary setting in Chapter 5).

Ask your loved ones to help you stick to your boundaries by reminding you that it's now family or social time and it's time you stopped working.

## Avoiding Cabin Fever

Did you escape from the corporate world and start out on your own because you wanted a better lifestyle and the freedom and flexibility of working on your own? Are you now finding that you miss the office banter and a chat with your work colleagues about last night's TV at the coffee machine?

An important part of running your own business and working from home is making sure that you don't go stir-crazy by disconnecting from the outside world. Depending on your type of business, you might have a lot of contact with clients and customers, or you may be rather isolated – perhaps spending much of your time working in your home office or out on the road, alone.

Here are a few ways to avoid cabin fever – that cooped-up, lonely feeling you get when you realise that the most meaningful conversation you've had all day is with the dog.

## *Joining in with networking*

There's nothing quite like spending time with other people to lift you out of feeling trapped, bored, or lonely. A great way to meet other people is to attend local networking events. There, you can connect with other home workers and develop a support system for your business.

More and more networking groups meet for breakfast, lunch, or in the evening, so find a time that suits you and talk to other like-minded people. Alternatively, start up your own network group and meet once a month for a social coffee, lunch, or evening drink – especially if the usual breakfast and evening meetings don't fit your schedule.

 To find networking groups in your area, check out your local Chamber of Commerce, Business Link, or do some research online.

## *Connecting online*

If face-to-face networking doesn't suit you, why not get involved in online networking? A rapidly expanding number of sites cater for both business and social networks – such as Facebook, LinkedIn, Ecademy, and Yahoo! groups. Not only can you exchange business ideas, get support, and build partnerships, but you also get the chance to let off steam.

Use Skype and Messenger 'chat' functions to interact with others in the same way you would take a break from work for a chat – don't get sucked in for hours! See Chapter 10 for more details on effectively managing your online time.

## *Changing the scene*

Escape from the phone and the Internet and go and find an 'office' away from your office. A local hotel can be ideal. Many of them have a lounge or bar area where you can plug in your laptop, access the Internet, and avoid the usual distractions of being at home.

You can find many places where you can get a coffee (or your drink of choice), sit with your laptop, a book, notes or writing materials, and have a couple of really productive hours while not getting interrupted by the phone, email, or other people (except when you want to order another coffee).

Moving to a different room in the house can help too. A change of scenery is as good as a rest and can stimulate your creativity.

Sometimes, a trip to the kitchen can seem to be a welcome change of scene. But just because the fridge is only a hop, skip, and a jump from your desk, don't be tempted to raid it too often. It's easy to snack more often at home than when you're in a traditional office setup – although at least you don't have the temptation of the vending machine and you can make yourself a decent cup of coffee!

## *Blowing away the cobwebs*

Taking frequent breaks during your working day is the best way to recharge those tired batteries. When you work from home, try to get out during your break – get out for some fresh air for a few minutes and reconnect with the world out-side your home office.

Getting out for some exercise can be a good way of taking a break during the day or when you've finished a number of tasks. This is where combining a few household activities can come in useful. Walk up to the corner shop for supplies or down to the post box, or just spend a few minutes out in the garden.

See Chapter 15 for more ideas on building exercise into your day. And remember: a change of pace and activity is as good as a rest too.

# *Forming Your Support Team*

Just because you work for yourself, doesn't mean that you're working on your own. Create your own support team – people you can go to for advice, inspiration, or just a chat.

You'll already have a few people that are an important part of your business:

- ✔ Accountant
- ✔ Bookkeeper
- ✔ Graphic designer
- ✔ IT support
- ✔ Printer
- ✔ Virtual assistant
- ✔ Web designer

In addition, you can put together your own research and development team made up of existing customers, friends, colleagues, or people you collaborate with. Ask them for feedback on your ideas or products or just for support. Test out new products or ideas on them.

Create a group of a few like-minded people, peers, or colleagues and meet up regularly, whether face to face or by phone, to discuss your current challenges, brainstorm ideas, share goals and progress, or just to support and motivate each other.

Several websites offer advice and resources for new businesses:

- ✔ www.businesslink.gov.uk
- ✔ www.startups.co.uk
- ✔ www.smallbusiness.co.uk
- ✔ www.hmrc.gov.uk/startingup/

Get together with a friend or colleague once a week or once a month and work together in the same space but on your own businesses. You'll be more focused as long as you don't distract each other; you can check in and keep each other motivated and you'll have someone to bounce ideas off and get feedback.

# Chapter 13

# Setting Up Your Home Office

· · · · · · · · · · · · · · · · · · · · · · · · · · · · · · · · · · · · · · · · · · ·

## In This Chapter

▶ Creating your work space

▶ Selecting office furniture

▶ Using technology

· · · · · · · · · · · · · · · · · · · · · · · · · · · · · · · · · · · · · · · · · · ·

*C*reating an office environment in your home helps you really get into 'work mode' and focus on your tasks. In this chapter, I show you how to set up a well-equipped, well-organised, and comfortable work space. By spending a little time creating a suitable work environment, you can work more smoothly and efficiently, and enjoy the flexibility of working from home without getting distracted and becoming unproductive.

Keep in mind that it's important to equip your home office with the essentials you need to run your business in a timely and efficient manner. At the start you may not be able to spend out money on brand new equipment but look at buying good quality second-hand furniture and storage units until you can buy new. Save your money for computer equipment and other essentials where new is best.

## Thinking About Your Work Space

The first thing you need is space to work in – an 'office' for yourself and your business. The following sections give you food for thought as you plan and organise your work space.

Let your office be inspiring and motivating, and reflect your personality. You can have a bit of fun – after all, you don't want it to be too boring and functional; you're working in your own space now and not in a big corporate office or cubicle.

## Creating your own space

Your work space needs to be clearly designated, and, ideally, separate. You may have to start with the dining room table but as soon as you can, get a work area that is a separate part of your home. Even if you only work from home occasionally, you're not going to be as productive if you're sitting on the sofa or spread out on the kitchen counter.

Create an 'office' – a space you can call your own. It's better to have your office in a separate room with a door than in a corner of the kitchen or living room. Ideally, your office should be a separate room where your working environment won't be disrupted by external forces like family members 'borrowing' things, or having to clear things away at mealtimes or when friends come to stay.

Why not set up your office in the garden shed! Yes, these days you can get some really lovely office space that essentially comes as a glorified shed and if you don't have a spare room in the house and you've got a reasonably sized garden, it can be an ideal solution. You have your own space, it's away from the main house so you can feel that you're 'going to work', and you can shut the door on it at the end of the day.

## Considering light

Natural daylight is important in any workspace, so it's no good setting up your office in the cupboard under the stairs. If you use a computer screen it's important to have a mix of natural and artificial light to make sure that your eyes don't get tired.

While you may not have the fluorescent, headache-inducing lighting of the office, or the stuffy air-conditioning, you also don't have Health and Safety or Compliance leaning over your shoulder making sure that you don't have too much glare on your screen.

Don't position your computer screen in direct sunlight or with your back to a window so the sun shines on your screen. Have a desk lamp for directional light and for reading.

## Minimising noise

Some elements of working from home aren't always compatible with running a business. You answer the phone with a crying baby under your arm and a toddler round your feet, the dog barking at the delivery man who's just turned up and rung the doorbell . . . and then your mobile phone rings.

Ideally, your work environment should be as quiet as possible. It's difficult to concentrate (and so work efficiently) if you're being distracted by noise. But when tranquillity isn't within reach, bear in mind the following:

- ✔ Unplug the phone or don't answer it if you're in the middle of a family crisis. This is where an answering machine or answering service comes in very useful.

- ✔ If you work in a noisy environment and you need a period of quiet time in which to work, go somewhere quiet such as the library, a local coffee shop, hotel, or even a friend's house.

- ✔ Background music or the radio on quiet can help block out unwanted noise. However, you may find that while you have one ear listening to the music or talking, your concentration isn't fully focused on what you're doing. So if the task needs all your attention or you want to get it done quickly, switch off the radio or music player.

- ✔ Invest in some earplugs to block-out background noise. They can make all the difference to your concentration!

## Avoiding clutter

Try to have a clear space to work in so you don't feel overwhelmed or distracted by things around you that aren't related to your work. Put things away after you've finished using them or that you don't immediately need – this applies both to your office and around the house.

---

## Home office basics

When setting up your home office, the basic essentials that you may need include:

- ✔ Back-up device
- ✔ Chair
- ✔ Computer (desktop or laptop)
- ✔ Desk
- ✔ Drawers
- ✔ Fax machine
- ✔ Filing cabinet
- ✔ Internet access
- ✔ Phone (landline and/or mobile)
- ✔ Printer/scanner
- ✔ Shelf unit
- ✔ Shredder
- ✔ Stationery items (see the shopping list in Chapter 7)
- ✔ Wastepaper basket

---

You don't need to work in a totally neat and uncluttered environment but if you're always losing valuable time sifting through piles of paper to find things, lose things, or have piles of unpaid bills or overdue accounts, check out Chapter 7 which gives you some pointers on how to improve your situation.

Make sure that the place where you work is functional with the things you use on a daily basis easily to hand so that you don't waste time searching for things.

Get into the habit of putting things back where they need to be. At the end of the day, spend a few minutes tidying up (little and often). If something needs to go upstairs, place it at the bottom of the stairs for the next time you go upstairs and vice versa. Do it when you think of it or see it and then you won't forget.

## *Keeping your space professional*

Do clients and customers need to visit you? Do you have a suitable, private space in which to meet them? Keep in mind remaining businesslike and professional. Not only does a pleasant meeting area create a good impression but it also helps you to feel more professional as you work.

# Choosing Office Furniture

Invest wisely in furniture that's practical, durable, and comfortable. You're going to spend a fair amount of your day in your home office, so you should be comfortable and have everything you need to hand to save time searching for it in other places in the house.

If you have limited space or work in the corner of a room, use office furniture that can be closed up or rolled away at the end of the day.

## Chair

Invest in a decent chair. Cheap and cheerful is all very well when you're starting out, but you'll regret it in the end when you're suffering from backache and fatigue.

Here are some things to look for when buying your office chair:

- ✔ **Adjustable seat:** Your feet should touch the ground.
- ✔ **Adjustable back:** For correct support for your spine when sitting or reclining.
- ✔ **Comfortable seat and padding:** If you're sitting for long periods of time.
- ✔ **Padded arm rests:** To reduce shoulder strain.
- ✔ **Swivel seat and casters:** So that you can move easily without twisting.

If you have a back problem, you can buy ergonomic back chairs in which you sit in a kneeling position. These cause less strain on your back but take some getting used to.

## Desk

Your desk should be a large enough area with space to work, lay out any papers, and set up your computer. Choose one with built-in drawers for stationery and papers, or buy a separate drawer unit.

## Checking your insurance

Be aware of insurance implications when using your own house for business purposes. If you have specialist equipment or have clients come to visit in your home, you need additional insurance for your business.

Advise your insurance company that you use your home for work. As long as you're not using it to make or store large quantities of materials and just as office space, it's not likely to be a problem, but do check first. And make sure that your office equipment is covered under your contents, or increase it as necessary.

It's better to keep as much as possible off the desk and away in drawers, storage boxes, stacking systems, and files. You save time and can be more efficient if you're not searching around for another pen or the stapler underneath a pile of papers.

Filing trays and folders can be used to sort paperwork on your desk as you work and can be put away at the end of the day (see Chapter 7 for more info).

## Storage units

One thing that's going to accumulate in your home office in the same way as any other office is the paperwork. You need to have a way of organising it and keeping your workplace manageable. Despite the revolution of the paperless office with the introduction of new technology, it's still a necessary part of any business.

You need a filing cabinet, drawers, or shelving for storing the paperwork, books, folders, and files you need at hand on a day-to-day basis. Keep everything organised by sorting through your files regularly. Clearing out old paperwork and placing it in archive boxes and files that can be safely stored away saves time by not having to search through old paperwork.

To cut down on the paper you're storing, think about scanning and saving files to CD or DVD.

Use the wall space too. Try whiteboard or pinboards for writing up your daily task list, displaying your goals, for notes, or contact info you need to reference or as a reminder – but don't let them become over-used and cluttered. See your year or month at a glance by using an A3 calendar and a few useful posters – either business-related, for inspiration, or a few favourite photos to liven up your work space.

# Taking on Technology

Technology is great for saving time, making your life easier and helping you to manage your time more effectively. The following sections outline the must-haves for your home office. (For more details on time-saving technology, look at Chapter 18.)

At home, you don't have the support of your company's IT department to come and help you out when things go wrong. So keep it simple. Try to be self-sufficient but also know what you're doing and use technology as a tool. This is where it's worthwhile paying a bit more for quality and reliability. The last thing you want is technology that lets you down and wastes time when it doesn't work.

## Phone

Two handsets are almost essential. You can guarantee that if you're upstairs, the phone that rings is downstairs. You rush downstairs to get the call and it rings off. If you're downstairs, the same Murphy's Law applies. If you have two or more handsets, as long as they're in their correct places, you'll spend less time dashing for the phone.

On the landline, having an answering machine lets you take control of your calls:

- ✔ You don't miss callers if you're away from the office.
- ✔ You can switch it on if you want some undisturbed time.
- ✔ You can screen your calls, and decide who to talk to and when.

Have a separate phone line for business if you need to. That way it's easier to switch off from work.

You may also need a mobile phone. Many mobiles now offer much more than just a way of keeping in touch while you're out of the office. Some mobiles also act as a PDA (Personal Digital Assistant) and can be used to access your contacts, calendar, notes, address book, and e-mails.

Don't become a slave to the phone – mobile or landline. You can, and should, switch off whichever phone you use for business calls when outside office hours.

# Computer

It's pretty likely that you're going to need a computer as part of your home office and it's going to be the most expensive piece of equipment you buy for your home office.

Either buy as high a specification as your budget can afford or go for a more basic specification and model and aim to upgrade every couple of years. And always buy as much memory as you can afford. It's what applications use to run and the more you run the slower the machine gets.

If technology is a key tool for your business, it's worth investing in something reliable.

### Desktop, laptop, or both?

Desktop computers are larger both in physical size and storage capacity. They have more disk space and memory and adapt more readily when it comes to making additions to them such as a separate keyboard and screen, mouse, external hard drives, speakers, and so on.

Desktops tend to be more rugged, last longer, and are easier to maintain than laptops. Laptops take a lot of battering when they're lugged around from place to place and can easily be stolen.

Laptops cost more for the same specification of desktop and are more expensive to repair if anything goes wrong, but you're paying for portability. However, you can use a docking station with your laptop. You plug your laptop into the docking station when you're at your desk, so that you can have a separate keyboard, mouse, and other devices – just like a desktop – which gives you greater flexibility and a better working position.

Desktops last longer because you can upgrade them. If one part fails, a desktop is easier to fix. If a laptop goes wrong you lose the whole thing while it's being repaired.

If you need to be mobile and have your technology with you wherever you are, then a laptop is ideal. Plug it in and you can work from pretty much anywhere and with WiFi technology (Wireless Internet) you can be connected to the Internet and read your email too.

Choose a brand that is reliable, lightweight, and with a good battery life so that you can continue to work on a long train journey or while away from the office in a meeting.

Get a spare battery to take with you so you can swap it over to extend the time you can work away from home or from a power source such as on a train journey or aeroplane.

### Putting your health and safety cap on

When you work in-house for a company, a health and safety person usually does a workstation assessment to check your computer is set up in the best possible way for you. When you work from home, you need to do that for yourself.

Have your screen at the right height – at eye level so that you're not straining your neck. Your keyboard should be at the right height so that your wrists are straight and your shoulders relaxed. Adjust your chair to the right height and angle depending on whether you're using the keyboard or writing.

Use an ergonomic mouse and keyboard if you're going to use your computer for long hours. Get an external mouse and keyboard if you have a laptop and a stand to raise the monitor up nearer to eye-level.

## Internet

Whatever you use the Internet for, it pays to have a fast broadband connection.

You can use the Internet to make phone calls using VoIP (Voice over Internet Protocol) on a broadband connection. This provides a low cost way of placing a call using a headset, or speaker and microphone, to other computers, or to landlines and mobiles.

Install anti-virus and firewall software to protect your computer from external hacking or malicious software and keep the software up-to-date.

## Printer

When choosing a printer, take into account the cost of consumables such as print cartridges, toner, and paper. The printer may be a great price but the cost of replacement cartridges may work out to be expensive, especially if you're using a colour printer. *Note:* Make sure that your printer uses separate colour cartridges or you end up wasting coloured ink when just one colour runs out.

Multi-function printers combine a printer, copier, scanner, and sometimes a fax machine in one device. If you're likely to use all these functions, consider buying a combined machine to save space in your office. However, be aware that if one function fails, you're likely to lose all the others too.

If you have any quantity of printing to do, consider using a local printing service. They produce great quality print for a lower cost than printing on your computer's printer, especially when you take into account the paper and ink or toner. Use your own printer for low volumes.

## Back-up facilities

What would be the impact to your business if you lost important data or your computer suddenly died? How would you function?

Be aware that the longer you have a computer, the more likely it is that at some point something is going to go wrong. A computer crash or loss of data can ruin a business. Therefore, it's essential to back up, back up, back up.

You can use CDs, DVDs, USB pens, external hard drives and online facilities to safely and quickly secure your data. Chapter 7 gives all the details on these back-up devices, and essential tips for backing up.

# Part V
# Looking at the Bigger Picture

"You can't beat the benefits of Time
Management—you should try it someday."

## In this part . . .

**D**o you feel that you're spending too much time at work and there must be more to life? Perhaps you'd like to improve your work – life balance?

The chapters in this part are aimed at enabling you to find time for your life. After all, the best benefit from effectively managing your time is finding more hours to spend with family, friends, and on your own doing whatever you please.

# Chapter 14

# Your Money or Your Life

*I*f you have a full-time job, you spend approximately 50 per cent of your waking hours at work – possibly more if you work for yourself. You might as well enjoy it and make the most of the time that you do spend working both in what you do and the people you work with.

This chapter is all about managing the time you spend earning money and how to ensure that you're working to live, rather than living to work. How do you score in those areas on your life balance wheel in Chapter 1?

Make sure that you're focusing on the important things in life like your partner, your children, and your health, and not just concentrating on work and money. If you spend too much time at work, you won't have any time for other things like family and friends.

## Getting Down to Business

Unless you're one of the lucky few with a country pad and Bentley at your disposal, you need to work in order to earn money to pay the bills and enjoy the lifestyle that you want to maintain. However, you don't need to allow work to rule your life. Rather, you can treat work as just part of what makes up your life.

# Wisdom from a mayonnaise jar

This story landed in my in-box and it really made me think, so I thought I'd share it with you.

A philosophy professor stood before his class, picked up a large empty mayonnaise jar, and proceeded to fill it with rocks. He asked the students if the jar was full and they agreed that it was.

The professor then poured a box of pebbles into the jar and shook it lightly. The pebbles rolled into the open areas between the rocks. He asked the students again if the jar was full. They agreed it was.

The professor poured a box of sand into the jar, which filled up the gaps between the pebbles. He again asked the students if the jar was full. The students responded with a unanimous 'yes'.

The professor then poured two cups of coffee into the jar, which was soaked up by the sand. The students laughed.

'Now', said the professor, 'I want you to recognise that this is your life. The rocks are the important things – your partner, your children, your family, your health, food and water. The pebbles are the other things that matter like your education, job, house, and your car. The sand is everything else. The small stuff like television, games, toys, sports, hobbies . . . email.

'If you put the sand into the jar first, there's no room for the pebbles or the rocks. The same goes for your life. If you spend all your energy and time on the small stuff, you'll never have room for the things that are important to you. Pay attention to the things that are critical to your happiness.

Take care of the rocks first – the things that really matter. Set your priorities. The rest is just sand.'

One of the students raised her hand and inquired what the coffee represented. The professor smiled. 'I'm glad you asked. It just goes to show you that no matter how full your life may seem, there's always room for coffee with a friend.'

British people work longer hours than their European counterparts. In the corporate world the' expectation is that if you're 'only' working 9 to 5, you're not working hard enough. Rather than being admired for being so organised that you get all your work done within your working hours, eyebrows are often raised if you leave on time.

People don't like to be the first to leave the office – even if they're not doing anything more productive than checking emails or shuffling paper around the desk. Others genuinely have so much work to do that they have to stay late to get it all done. Even if you're not paid overtime you can easily get into the bad habit of working late. Chapter 5 explains how not to say yes to everything the boss throws at you.

If you run your own business, you may be in the habit of working longer hours than you would if you were working for someone else, simply because it's your own business.

Plan your time appropriately and effectively. How many hours do you work, and how many hours do you want to work?

Part III is full of tips about how to adjust your workload so that you can better manage your time.

## *Loving what you do*

What does your work or business mean to you? Is it just the means to an end or your life-long passion? Although not everyone is lucky enough to have a job that they absolutely love or are working in an area that they're passionate about, you can do many things to get more out of your career.

Every now and then take a metaphorical step back from your job or your business and ask yourself if your work satisfies you. You don't want to get to retirement and wish you'd tried something else or done things differently, such as spending more time with the family. Keep your skills up to date. Set aside time to work on your career and plan in your training and ongoing development.

If your job isn't enjoyable and fulfilling, do you need to change career or simply change something about the way you currently work? Think about what's working and what's not and look at making a few changes.

Put a plan in place to improve your existing career or business prospects, gain promotion, or plan your retirement. Create a training and development plan with your boss. Identify the steps you need to take, skills you need to develop, or targets you need to achieve in order to progress your career or business. Look at where you'd like to be in two, five, or ten years' time.

Perhaps a concern of yours at work is your relationship with your manager, and other colleagues. You spend so much time with your colleagues, you need to get on with them on a day-to-day basis.

Get to know your colleagues better. What makes them tick? They have their own thoughts, dreams, and aspirations that probably aren't so different from yours. They go home at the end of the day to their lives outside of work.

Seeing a different side to people can give you a greater sense of respect for them. I'm not suggesting that you have to become best buddies with your boss, but try seeing things from his or her point of view every now and then to improve your relationship.

## Heading for the horizon: Your long-term view

Living from day to day is fine but sometimes you need to have a plan in mind to keep you focused on long-term goals.

Set clear goals at work about what you want to get done, not only each day but month by month and each year.

Take responsibility for your own career or business. Where do you want to be a year from now, and three years from now? Set a goal, such as:

- ✔ 'Next year, I want to get promoted.'
- ✔ 'In three years' time, I want to be at manager level.'

Then set some specific steps to get you there.

Make sure that you get feedback from your boss and your peers on your progress at work, which can help you to improve. You also get more job satisfaction if you know what you're aiming for. If you want to take your career or your business up a gear get yourself a mentor, someone you respect who's where you want to be or who's done what you want to do. This person can be someone at work or outside of work. Meet up with your mentor a few times a year to find out how she got where she is and to discuss your progress and what plans and actions you need to put into place.

If you're looking for a new career or want to use your existing job to jump into something different, spend some time thinking about what you want from your work. Use your existing work as a stepping stone to get you to where you want to be. You may not start out in the perfect job but concentrate on making the most of what you've got as well as planning your next move.

 Add to your skills and abilities. Go on training courses to help you progress at work. What are the things you're good at, what sort of work do you like to do? How can you create your perfect job?

# Sorting Out Money Matters

Money, although necessary, isn't the be all and end all. You can be earning a top salary but still not be happy. Or perhaps you spend all your hours at work in order to earn the money you need to support your lifestyle.

Review your life wheel (in Chapter 1) from the perspective of having no money and having plenty of money. You may find that certain areas relating to personal relationships, health, and family remain pretty much the same. The important things in life aren't dependent on how much you earn, although I can't deny that money gives you freedom of choice and a better lifestyle, including more time to do the things you enjoy and less time fretting over the bills.

## Working out what your time is worth

If you work for a living, then during working hours your time is money. You may be less inclined to fritter time away on things that add no value if you know the real cost to you (and your boss!) of this wasted time.

Working out your hourly rate makes you think more clearly about how valuable your time is. Here's how to calculate what a working hour is worth for you:

1. **Work out your weekly rate.**

   To do so, take your annual income (your salary or your self-employment earnings) and divide it by the number of weeks you work (excluding holiday time).

   For example: £23,500 ÷ 47 = £500 per week (allowing for 5 weeks' holiday)

2. **Work out your hourly rate.**

   To do so, divide your weekly rate from Step 1 by the average number of hours you work in a week.

   For example: £500 ÷ 40 hours (per week) = £12.50 per hour

Re-do your calculation when you've had a pay rise or a change in income to keep your hourly rate up-to-date.

You now know what your hourly rate is. This can be a useful guide when you're looking at how you spend your time. You know what your time is worth, so you're better equipped to assess the value of doing a task. You may decide that your time is best spent elsewhere, and say no to a task (see Chapter 5) or delegate it to someone else (refer to Chapter 11).

## *Improving your finances*

Unless you're in the fortunate position of having more money than you know what to do with and have wisely invested for your future and old age, you may need help to improve your finances. Set aside some time to answer these questions:

- ✔ Do I spend more than I earn, less than I earn, or about the same?
- ✔ Is my credit card debt more than I can handle (be honest)?
- ✔ Do I manage to save on a regular basis?
- ✔ Do I spend for the long-term or short-term?
- ✔ How well do I manage my expenses, investments, and savings?

# *Income versus outgoings*

Knowing how much money you have coming in and going out helps you to be better organised and saves you time not having to worry about your finances, wondering if you've enough money to pay the bills, or spending time juggling funds at the end of each month. Put a structure in place to help plan and organise your finances.

- ✔ **Start a money diary.** If you're not sure where your money is going, make a note of everything you spend in the week – from the smallest amount to the biggest bill – every newspaper, coffee, snack, and bus fare. At the end of the week tot up how much you've spent.

- ✔ **Work out your monthly expenditure.** Gather your bank statements, credit card bills, household bills – everything that goes out. List your sources of income – payslips from full-time jobs and part-time work. Is your income sufficient for your outgoings?

- ✔ **Reduce your spending.** Check your bank statements – are you paying for things that you no longer need? Are you getting the best rate on insurance and utility bills?

- ✔ **Start saving.** Set aside at least 10 per cent of your income each month and put it into a separate savings account. Use your savings for emergencies, holidays, unexpected expenses, or simply as a buffer.

- ✔ **Dig direct debit.** Pay all your regular, monthly expenses by direct debit to save time and pay bills on time. You won't have to miss a payment, get unnecessary charges, or risk being cut off by utilities providers.

- ✔ **Use your cheque stubs.** When you write a cheque enter the amount and what it's for on the stub – you won't forget what you paid for a few weeks later when your bank statement arrives. Do the same with credit card receipts.

- ✔ **Pay off your credit card in full each month.** Avoid overspending and those high interest rates.

- ✔ **Keep receipts for all your spending.** Keep your receipts in a folder so you can quickly check them against your bank statement.

---

# Financially savvy surfing

Check out the following websites for more money advice:

✔ Tips for saving money with regular updates and offers: www.moneysavingexpert.com.

✔ Price comparison sites for all utilities, shopping, and insurance: www.moneysupermarket.com and www.pricerunner.co.uk.

✔ Free debt advice from the Citizen's Advice Bureau: www.citizensadvice.org.uk.

✔ News and information on personal finance from the Motley Fool: www.fool.co.uk.

---

## *Managing your money*

After you've worked out where your money goes, stay in control. Set aside time each week to sit down and go through your personal expenses and get your finances in order. You only need a few minutes to sort through your receipts, pay any bills, file away invoices and statements – and this saves time in the long run. Improve your planning and create some regular money habits so you're far better organised and avoid the stress of overspending or missing payments.

Once a month, go through your statements and balance your credit card receipts and any cheque book stubs. Record all your income and outgoings as you go, so you know just what you're spending. A simple spreadsheet does the trick.

If you have business expenses to handle, set aside the time to go through the books updating invoices and receipts. If you don't like doing the books, find a bookkeeper or accountant to do them for you each month, which saves you time. Chapter 7 gives you more ideas on keeping your accounts organised, which certainly saves you time in the long run.

Book the time out for checking your finances in your diary for the same time each week – perhaps on a Friday. You may need to set aside a couple of hours or half-a-day once a week, until you're more organised. You can't create new habits overnight, so give yourself a few months to settle in, and then just check your finances for an hour or so once a month.

## Doing an annual review

Once a year, it's worth taking time out to have a review of your personal finances whether it's on your own or with the help of a financial adviser to make sure that things are in order. Go through what you've spent over the year.

Use this checklist once a year. Put a reminder in your calendar or organiser for right at the end or the beginning of the year.

✔ Review all your Direct Debits and standing orders. Cancel any that you no longer need, such as membership fees, magazine subscriptions, and so on.

✔ Review your utility bills – gas, electricity, phone – are you getting the best rates? Look around and switch if you need to.

✔ Check that your current bank account is paying you the best rate of interest.

✔ Have a savings account that pays you the highest rate of interest available.

Banks often offer a good rate to new accounts but then drop the rate over the following years. Keep on top of these changes and switch regularly.

✔ Review your savings. Are they in the best place? Have they grown enough to be put into an investment plan?

✔ Review any investments. Are they performing well – or is it time to switch to a new or different type of investment?

Apathy can cost you time and money. Take time once a year to make sure that you're properly managing your personal money, so you don't waste time throughout the year having to sort things out.

For more information on all things related to personal finance, read *Sorting Out Your Finances For Dummies*, 2nd Edition, by Melanie Bien (Wiley).

# Chapter 15

# Looking After Yourself

*O*ne of the important aspects of finding extra time in your day is that you now have time to exercise which means improved health.

If you're fit and healthy you're likely to have more energy, be better able to concentrate, and be more productive and less stressed.

Regular exercise benefits your general health by increasing your energy levels, reducing stress, and lifting your mood. However busy you may be – find time to get active every day.

Plan time to look after yourself both physically and mentally. You need quiet 'me-time' every now and then. Take time just for you to do exactly what you want, whether relaxing in the bath with a good book or going for a walk to meet friends.

## Being a Picture of Health

You can achieve better health by exercising regularly and eating a healthy, balanced diet.

If finding the time to exercise is a problem, think about how important your health is to you. Once you make your health a priority, finding the time to look after yourself becomes more important. Getting fit and healthy doesn't mean you have to become a gym bunny and spend hours preparing healthy meals. This section gives you tips, tricks, and shortcuts to better health.

## Enjoying exercise

Sensible exercise is about increasing your general activity in everyday activities, finding exercise that you enjoy, and making reasonable time to do so without stress.

Any activity over and above what you do normally burns up additional calories.

To feel the benefit without feeling the burn, get your heartrate up for between 20–30 minutes, three times a week.

Fit exercise into your day, whether at the beginning or end of your day or during your lunch-break if you have somewhere near to work where you can exercise.

Here are just a few ideas that don't require expensive equipment or gym membership, and don't leave you hot, sweaty, and exhausted. You can do these exercises in the middle of a workday and still go back to work without having to shower.

### Walking

Running may not be for everyone but walking is enjoyable for most people and is a very effective exercise.

Get outside in the fresh air at lunch-time and give your legs a stretch. Walk to the shops instead of taking the bus. If you have a local park, take a brisk 20-minute walk in your lunch-break.

Go for a longer walk at the weekend. Take the rest of the family along or go out with a friend. You don't have to do a great trek, just an hour or so of brisk walking.

### Pedal power

If you have a short journey to make to work or to the shops, why not cycle? It's free, quicker than walking, and great exercise. And who needs the expense and inconvenience of parking?

Kit yourself out with a helmet, rucksack for essentials and valuables, and don't forget lights if you're going out after dark.

### Swimming

Swimming is a cheap and fun form of exercise – you just need a swimming costume and of course, a nearby pool. Swimming is a great way to exercise because it supports your body weight, is kinder to the joints than load-bearing exercises such as running and aerobics, and it works all the major muscle groups.

A few minutes swimming lengths is a good way to set yourself up for the day or to unwind after a busy day.

### Stretching and toning

If you want gentle exercise, try yoga, tai chi, or pilates. Tai chi is a very gentle form of exercise, based on movement and balance through a series of flowing pattern of movements. Pilates helps to develop core stability, which is important for a strong back and a flat stomach. Both are great for toning, flexibility, and strength, and are suitable for all ages and abilities. Find a class you can go to before or after work or even in your lunch-break.

After you've grasped the basics, you need minimal equipment for these exercise techniques, and you only need to find a few minutes to do them during the day, in the evening, or first thing in the morning.

## Psyching up for cycling

It takes me about 20 minutes to drive into my town. I spend 5 to 10 minutes finding somewhere to park, which may or may not be close to where I'm going, so I might need another 10 minutes to walk there. So driving into town can take me an hour and then of course I have to pay for parking.

If I cycle, it takes me about 30 minutes. I can get directly to where I'm going. All I need to do is lock the bike to the nearest lamppost or bike park. I've arrived more quickly than driving and had some great exercise to boot!

Cycling isn't something I'd chose to do in bad weather but definitely saves time and hassle when the weather's fine.

## Getting active

As well as finding time for specific exercise, think about what you do on a daily basis and find ways to build more activity into your day as you go about your normal routine. Increasing your general activity is a lot easier than trying to fit in an hour or two to go to the gym or attend an exercise class.

Here are just a few ideas to get more activity into your everyday life:

- ✔ **Leave the car behind.** Think carefully before you hop in the car to go somewhere or to run an errand. Got a letter to post? Walk to the nearest post box. Popping to the shop? Take sturdy bags and walk it.

- ✔ **On the buses.** Get off the bus a couple of stops earlier than you need to and walk the extra distance.

- ✔ **Park and walk.** If you really have to drive, park farther away from work or the shops than necessary and enjoy the additional exercise you get from the extra walk.

- ✔ **Housework.** You may hate doing it, but cleaning, dusting, vacuuming, and washing the car all increase your level of activity and get your heartrate going. Now there's a reason for doing the housework!

- ✔ **Gardening.** An hour or so of weeding, mowing the lawn, and digging is great exercise. If you really want a workout, mow the lawn with a manual lawnmower. Use hand shears instead of a strimmer to do the edges of flowerbeds and lawns.

- ✔ **Use the stairs.** Climbing stairs is great exercise and may even be quicker than taking a lift that stops at every floor. Unless you live or work in a skyscraper, always take the stairs.

- ✔ **School run.** If you're within walking distance from your local school, walk your children to school. Not only do you all get some exercise but you also have some chatting and playing time on the way back.

- ✔ **Ditch the remote.** Get up to change television channels – it's not exactly a strenuous workout but at least it prevents you from sitting in one position for the whole evening.

Some of these activities require you to plan your time a bit and be a little more organised. Leave yourself a few minutes more than you usually need so that you won't need to jump in the car because you've run out of time.

# Taking Time for Healthy Eating

When you're busy, you often don't have time to eat properly and end up grabbing a snack during the day, eating at your desk, or even skipping meals altogether.

At the end of the day, reaching for a ready-meal or grabbing a take-away on the way home is easier than preparing a healthy meal.

Or so it seems. You may think that you don't have enough time to cook and prepare a healthy meal but with a little fore-thought and planning, it's possible.

## At home

Breakfast really is the most important part of the day. If you need to, get up a few minutes earlier so that you can have a healthy breakfast. Oat-based cereals such as muesli and porridge fill you up and provide energy all morning – much healthier than grabbing a coffee and a Danish on the way to work.

Eat a balanced diet with plenty of wholefoods (unprocessed and unrefined foods) such as brown bread, pasta, rice, grains and pulses, fresh fruit and vegetables, fish, fresh meat, nuts, and seeds, which are naturally higher in vitamins and minerals from over refined and processed food.

Keep everything in moderation. Keep fatty and sugary foods to a minimum but if you enjoy chocolate, cakes, and curries there's nothing wrong with eating them every once in a while, just not every night! Think 80/20. Eat healthily 80 per cent of the time and enjoy yourself the other 20 per cent!

Take the time to eat every 2–3 hours throughout the day – little and often – to avoid your blood sugar fluctuating too much, which can result in a dip in energy that makes you feel tired, light-headed, and shaky. Have a couple of oatcakes or a banana with you to eat as a snack. Don't eat a heavy meal late in the evening. Your body is naturally slowing down and food is harder to digest.

Here's a happy host of tips to inspire you to make time for healthy eating at home:

- ✔ Have a cooking day at the weekend and make up a batch of meals for later in the week. A few hours of cooking can create a whole range of meals such as pasta sauce, chilli, lasagne, shepherds pie, casseroles, stews. You can cook up mince and freeze it for use in chillies, lasagne, or as a pasta sauce.

- ✔ Make double the amount when you cook, and freeze in meal-sized portions for later when you need a home-made ready-meal. Take out the frozen meal in the morning, place it in the fridge, and it's ready to heat up when you get home.

- ✔ Try recipes that give you more than one meal. If you cook a big joint on Sunday you can use the leftover meat for cold meat, casserole, stir-fry or risotto, and soup on subsequent days.

- ✔ Stir-fries and pasta are quick to prepare. You can prepare and cook a meal from scratch in 15 minutes. Use your imagination – recipe books have plenty of ideas for quick and easy meals that don't take much longer than half-an-hour to prepare and cook.

- ✔ Keep stocked up on the basics so you're always able to produce a good, healthy meal in a matter of minutes. Store pasta, tinned tomatoes, beans, eggs, cheese, and frozen vegetables.

Preparing and cooking a meal is a good way to unwind after a hard day at work. Look on cooking as something pleasurable to be enjoyed rather than as a chore.

Plan your meals at the beginning of the week and shop accordingly. You save time by planning because you won't have to waste time thinking of what to eat every evening and popping to the shop for the missing ingredient.

## Becoming a water baby

Being dehydrated affects your energy levels and productivity, and you feel tired and sluggish. The majority of people don't drink as much as recommended during the day. If you're thirsty, you're already dehydrated. Aim to drink at least a 1.2 litres of fluid a day; that's 6 to 8 small (200ml) glasses. Drink more if it's hot and definitely more if you're exercising.

Upping your water intake isn't that hard – you just need to get into the habit. Drink a glass of water first thing in the morning and last thing at night.

Carry a bottle of water around with you so you always have it to hand and keep it topped up. Have a bottle on your desk and one in the car. Ask for a glass of water when you order your coffee. Eat fruit and veg that have a high water content

Other fluids like fruit juices (but watch the sugar) and herbal tea count towards your daily fluid intake but avoid caffeine and alcohol because these are diuretics and they dehydrate you faster.

## *At work*

Make sure that you take time for a proper lunch-break. Grabbing a sandwich and eating it at your desk isn't good for your stress or your digestion. You're far better off taking half-an-hour away from your desk instead of trying to work and eat at the same time. (Refer to Chapter 4 for more about how to organise your time.)

 Taking in your own lunch to work helps you to resist the temptation for unhealthy eating – at least you know what's going into the sandwich you've prepared. Rice and pasta-based salads or chopped vegetables such as carrots, peppers, and cucumbers are ideal for a healthy lunch.

Plan your lunch-time meals in advance and they'll only take a few minutes to prepare each morning. Take fruit into work rather than making a trip to the snack machine, which is probably full of crisps, chocolate, and biscuits (fat, fat, sugar, sugar).

If you don't make your own packed lunch, opt for the healthier meals or salads in the restaurant or cafeteria and don't have a large, heavy meal full of fat and carbohydrates such as pastry and potatoes at lunch-time. Stodgy meals make you feel more tired in the afternoon and your productivity drops. Go for protein (chicken, fish, cheese, eggs) and vegetables or salad and soup.

Here are some healthy snack ideas for work instead of chocolate and crisps:

- ✔ Fruit, such as apples and bananas, or dried fruit, such as raisins and apricots
- ✔ Oatcakes and crackers
- ✔ Nuts and seeds
- ✔ Raw vegetables such as carrots, celery, peppers, and cucumber

# Feeling Cool, Calm, and Collected

Stress isn't necessarily a bad thing. You need a certain level of stress to give you the motivation to get things done and meet your deadlines.

## Tutti-frutti

I used to have a fruit bowl at work because a) it was a good way to reach my 5-a-day fruit and veg targets and b) I wasn't tempted to reach for a chocolate bar when my energy levels dipped.

My work colleagues also thought the fruit bowl was a great idea. Not only would they come and visit me more often but they also started bringing their own contributions, so we had a regular supply of whatever was in season – apples, grapes, strawberries, cherries, and bananas.

If my colleagues happened to find the fruit bowl empty, they were always disappointed and I knew I'd improved their eating habits as well as mine!

However, prolonged periods of stress can have a serious impact on your health, affecting your performance and causing physical, emotional, and mental problems. These problems include back, neck, and shoulder stiffness, stomach upsets, mood swings, lack of concentration, forgetfulness, headaches, anxiety, and depression. If you don't find time to relax, you can end up spending more time being ill or recovering from illness – not the best use of your time.

Find different ways to manage and relieve your stress. Start out by eating a healthy, balanced diet and getting regular exercise (described in the preceding sections). The time you take to do both more than pays off in the long run.

- ✔ Avoid using stimulants to de-stress such as coffee, tea, cigarettes, and alcohol. You may think that these help you relax but they have their own downside. Over time you need more to have the same effect. Tea, coffee, and alcohol are diuretics and disrupt sleep patterns when taken in large quantities. Cigarettes are addictive.

- ✔ Allow time for yourself, your family, and friends. Take a few minutes of the day for yourself but also make sure that you're spending time with those close to you (see Chapter 16).

- ✔ Take up meditation or breathing exercises to help you relax (see the sidebar 'Chilling out with simple breathing exercises'). Switching off from the external world for a few minutes is very calming. Your local alternative therapy or Buddhist centre can help, and take a look at *Meditation For Dummies* by Stephan Bodian and Dean Ornish (Wiley).

- ✔ Take responsibility for your own situation and don't worry about things that are outside of your control. If you don't like things the way they are, only you have the power to change them.

Got a knotty problem? Go for a walk. Walking or running is a right-brained activity. As the Romans said, *solvitas perambulum* – solve it while you walk. Take a break from your left-brained, logical thinking processes (refer to Chapter 1). Use the time to allow your brain to do its thing, solving problems, while you get the additional benefit of some exercise. See the later section 'Exercising your mind' for more tips.

## Chilling out with simple breathing exercises

You only have to type 'correct breathing' into an Internet search engine to find myriad claims about the effects of good breathing – from eliminating asthma to helping with obesity and depression. Whatever the truth of these claims, the simple fact is that deep breathing is a quick, effective, and drug-free way to relax your mind and body.

Most people only use the top part of their lungs when they breathe. To breathe correctly you need to use the whole of your lungs.

✔ Breathe deeply into your stomach for a count of two, then into your upper chest for two counts to fully inflate your lungs.

✔ Reverse the process and breathe out for four counts.

Try this for a few minutes at any time throughout the day to revive your body. Use it as a warm-up when exercising or walking. Matching your breathing with your stride is a great fat-burner as you breathe more deeply, use your stomach muscles and oxygenate your blood, which raises your metabolism.

If you're feeling nervous or stressed, perhaps before giving a talk in an unfamiliar situation, take ten slow, deep breaths to calm you.

Sleep is important to help your body recover from the day, de-stress, and relax. If you're not getting the sleep you need, you're likely to reach for that cup of coffee every morning to keep you going. Lack of sleep affects the brain more than the body – like stress, lack of sleep has a negative effect on your mood, concentration, and memory. Long periods without sleep can affect health and has been known to increase the risk of heart disease.

Set a regular time for going to bed and getting up, and stick to it. Your body likes routine. You need to get between 6–10 hours of sleep a night. If you feel tired after only six hours sleep, or sluggish if you sleep for too long, find the optimum for you (usually between 7–8 hours) and get that on at least four nights a week. People tend to need less sleep as they get older and some people can survive on less sleep than others, so find out what works for you.

# Climbing the Beanstalk of Personal Growth

One of the important aspects of good time management is that you free up some time for yourself. All work and no play is no fun at all!

Personal growth is the process of acquiring new skills, replacing bad habits with good ones, and using your strengths and developing your weaknesses to make the most of who you are.

Think about your personal and work life:

- ✔ What new skill would you like to develop?
- ✔ Do you have an activity you'd like to try?
- ✔ Do you have a habit you'd like to change?
- ✔ What are you tolerating in your life, work, and environment?

Everyone has areas where they'd like to improve. In your work or business you probably spend time mastering new skills and keeping on top of the latest developments in regulations, products, or technology, but how often do you spend time on your personal development?

## Listening to your body

Your body often tells you when something isn't right. You're more likely to get colds, headaches, and stomach problems when you're under stress and your immune system is low.

If you don't feel right, don't ignore it. Seek advice and get professional help or do something to correct the cause. For example, if you get a lot of backache, exercise to strengthen your core stability, and improve your posture.

Don't raid the medicine cabinet at the first sign of illness. Work out what caused the problem and give your body a chance to heal itself.

## Exercising your mind

You need to exercise your brain just as much as your body – use it or lose it! The more you use your brain, the more alert you'll stay.

Your brain has a left and right side. The left brain is associated with words, logic, numerical analysis, sequences and lists – it's the intellectual, 'business' side of your brain.

The right brain is associated with rhythm, spatial awareness, dimension, imagination, daydreaming, and colour and is the creative, emotional side of your brain.

To exercise your mind you need to use both sides of the brain. Imagine running a race with one arm and leg tied together behind your back. That's what most people do all the time with their brains. Here are a few ideas to give your brain a workout:

- ✔ Try brain teasers like crosswords, sudoku, IQ tests, and word puzzles to exercise your grey cells.

- ✔ If you usually use one side of your brain in your working life, try something that uses the other side of your brain.

- ✔ If you work with numbers try a drawing or painting class.

- ✔ If you have a creative job try logic puzzles, crosswords, and number games.

Whether you're left- or right-handed, try using your non-dominant hand for tasks like cleaning your teeth, using your mouse, and the phone, or even writing and drawing. Doing so feels awkward and uncomfortable at first, but your brain starts to make new connections in the process. If you keep practising, using the 'wrong' arm becomes easier.

Improve your memory by applying the tips and tricks that professional memory champions use to remember decks of cards, sequences of numbers, names, and faces:

- ✔ **Tell stories.** Create a story out of a list of items you want to remember such as bread, milk, and eggs. Link the words together using pictures, sound, and smell and make it as strong an image and story as possible – the sillier the better. For example, a loaf of bread is milking a cow that's standing on four eggs.

✔ **Try association.** Select an image to associate with the concept, name, or word you want to remember and then create images to link these words together. For longer or less familiar words, break the word down phonetically and create an image for each part of the word. Use exaggeration and action to make the image more memorable and then link the images together again using movement and activity.

✔ **Go on a journey.** Remember items by associating them with rooms in your house or objects or landmarks in a place or on a journey you know well, such as your route to work. Then create an image for each item you want to remember and associate it with the room or an object along the journey.

For a full explanation of these and other tips, take a look at *Use Your Memory* by Tony Buzan (BBC).

Invest time doing something different every week that takes you away from your usual routine:

✔ Take a different route to work.

✔ Try something new to eat.

✔ Don't watch TV for a week.

✔ Read a different type of book or magazine than your usual choice.

✔ Do your shopping in a different shop.

Engage all your senses – become more aware of your surroundings and notice the sights, sounds, smells, and perhaps even taste of your environment.

## Trying new things

You've no doubt heard the saying that you can't teach an old dog new tricks. Well, that's just an excuse. As you get older you may become more set in your ways but that doesn't mean you can't acquire new skills. Developing a new skill may take a little longer than when you were younger but all you need is commitment, focus, and, of course, practice.

Take a moment to think about something you've always wanted to do, such as playing a musical instrument, studying a new language, or trying a new sport or activity. Ask in your local library or adult education centre for the range of courses available as day and evening classes or workshops. Look online for online courses available by email or download. Check the cards and ads often displayed in cafés, shops, and therapy rooms.

Don't take on a new activity when you don't have the time to commit to it. You'll only become overwhelmed and frustrated. Make sure that you've cleared your priorities so that you have time for your new interests.

# Chapter 16

# Taking Time for Fun and Friends

*I*f you don't make time to have fun in your life, you're obviously working far too hard, even with all the tips and advice in this book!

If your work-life balance wheel in Chapter 1 shows that you need to be focusing on having fun and being with friends and family, then this chapter is for you. Set aside some time to see what you can do to bring these areas up to a 10 or at least improve where you are at the moment.

Are you having enough fun in your life? Do you flit from one event to another like a giggling socialite or do you spend all your weekends catching up on the chores you didn't have time for in the week? This chapter can help you find the balance.

When you become busy, these areas of your life tend to take second priority to work. In fact, these are the areas that can support you in your work. Friends and family can be sympathetic when you're going through a tough patch and having fun is a good way to let off steam and de-stress after a busy week at work.

# What Rocks Your Boat?

Have you ever really considered what you truly enjoy doing? Take a moment to reflect on your idea of fun. Fun for you may be:

- Doing hobbies.
- Exercising.
- Going to the cinema, theatre, or concerts.
- Playing sport.
- Relaxing.
- Trying something new, perhaps at an evening class.

How do you know when you're having fun and what does it mean to you? Everyone has a different idea of fun and enjoyment, so there's no right answer to this question, just what works for you.

Make a list of fun things to do. To start you off, here's a list of fun things that I like to do:

- Go for a walk, maybe to the beach or the woods.
- Cook a special meal.
- Play a game.
- Go for a picnic.
- Arrange a weekend away.
- Stay in bed all morning with a good book.
- Go to see my favourite band.
- Meet up with friends.

Take a look at your list and find time in your week or at least once a month to have more fun and do one of these things.

## You don't have to be mad to work here, but it helps

If you're so busy working, or if you spend long hours commuting to and from work, you may find that you're too tired at the end of the day to even think about going out in the evening. You may feel that you don't have enough time or money to have fun. Many people end up cramming too much into their weekend, exhausting themselves and starting the week tired.

A change is as good as rest. You can add a little fun into your working life by taking breaks during the day. Switch between different types of activity. If you've spent a few hours at the computer, make a few phone calls. If you've been working with words all day, try something with numbers.

Business doesn't have to be serious, so find ways of bringing a little fun and light-heartedness into your workplace too. This doesn't mean flicking elastic bands at your work colleagues or playing practical jokes but perhaps:

- Have a charity day where you get sponsored for doing something silly.

- Celebrate national days – dress up and bring in food.

- Get your team involved in a community project.

- Introduce a bit of humour – share jokes or cartoons.

- Go for a picnic lunch in a local park.

- Buy cakes for your team on your birthday.

- Arrange a night out – just for a drink or maybe a trip to the theatre, racecourse, or other event.

Lighten up – put a little more fun into your working day.

# Taking Time Out

How regularly do you take time out for yourself – to go and do something *you* really enjoy and that's purely for fun? Fun is an area of your life that can get out of balance if you let it.

If you don't make time to have fun then it's all too easy to let time slip away. You suddenly realise that you haven't seen your friends in ages – you've been too busy working. You haven't been to the cinema or theatre for months and when was the last time you went away for a weekend?

Even if you're very busy, taking time out is important because if you push yourself too hard you end up worn out, stressed, and ill. Take time out for the important things in your life and have some fun.

Humour is a great way to relax at the end of the day – or at any time for that matter. Laughter is a great stress reliever and, like exercise, releases endorphins, natural feel-good chemicals released by the brain to give you the feeling of well-being, relaxation, and a natural high. Laughing also improves your immune system and can be highly contagious! If you have a long commute to and from work, listen to an audio of your favourite funny book or comedy programme.

Do you have any hobbies? If not, why not develop a few? Think of an instrument you'd like to take up playing. Consider taking a painting or foreign language class. You can obtain details of your local adult education classes from your local library or enquire at your nearest college.

Make a point of going out at least once a week or sign up for a weekly evening class to tackle something new – or just try something different.

## Having a Break

Make sure that you plan in breaks throughout the year – not only a traditional main holiday once a year but frequent breaks. If you're working hard, you probably end up unwinding the first few days of your two-week holiday, and then spend the remainder of the time enjoying your holiday.

If you can afford it, try to plan three holidays a year. Doing so may sound like a luxury or you may think that you don't have the time, but you owe it to yourself. After a good break, you're relaxed and more focused. Book the time out at the beginning of the year. That way you can plan your time around your holidays and not feel that you have to squeeze in a break when you can.

You don't have to choose expensive foreign holidays. Plenty of low-cost breaks are available, such as camping, self-catering at off-peak times, or going on a volunteering break with BTCV (British Trust for Conservation Volunteers www2.btcv.org.uk), local Wildlife Trusts (www.wildlifetrusts.org.uk), or the National Trust (www.nationaltrust.org.uk). Maybe you prefer to get away for a few weeks each year and do something totally different. Or you may just want to spend time with family and friends, relaxing on a beach. Perhaps your holiday plans include relaxing with your partner, finding activities for the children, or just chilling out on your own. Whatever your reason, make sure that you make the most of your holiday time.

✔ Plan a main two-week holiday in the summer or winter.

✔ Take a couple of weeks at either end of the year.

✔ Arrange a few long weekends away.

✔ Do something special on the Bank Holiday weekends.

✔ Take a spontaneous day off work.

✔ Plan an afternoon off.

All these holidays – long and short – help to break up the year and a change of scenery is invigorating.

When you're going away on holiday avoid the temptation to take work with you. You work long and hard enough during the year so leave it all behind. Follow the tips and information in Chapter 11 and you'll be able to go on holiday knowing that everything is up to date and your work is in good hands until you come back refreshed from your break.

# Nurturing Family and Friendships

You may think that your family is always there but it's easy to neglect them. You find that you keep meaning to give them a call but keep putting it off. Maybe your closest friends have moved away and you don't see them as often as you'd like.

Make sure that you spend time focusing on the important people in your life and don't forget them just because you're busy. Relaxing and unwinding with friends is a good way to get back a sense of perspective and a little balance in your life.

Plan time in your diary and arrange to meet up with friends on a regular basis. Decide that you're going to go out socially once a week or entertain a group of friends once a month.

# Making Friends with Technology to Keep in Touch

Technology has improved communication no end. It's easy to pick up the phone to say 'hi' or to send a quick email. You can email friends on the other side of the world and stay in touch with social networking sites such as Facebook and MySpace, even though you may be hundreds or even thousands of miles apart.

Phone calls are a cheap and easy way of keeping in touch and quite often free within the UK. Even international calls don't have to cost the earth with competition for free or very low-cost services. Voice-over Internet phones enable you to call people from your computer as long as you've got a headset and microphone.

Try Skype (www.skype.com) for free software that runs over a broadband connection and provides free calls to other Skype users.

Install a software package that enables you to chat with friends so that you can keep in touch online and in real time. Most mail providers now have this feature available.

Mobile phones mean that you can keep in touch on the move and texts are easy and quick to send when you don't have time for a longer call.

Follow these tips for making time for your friends and family:

- ✔ Pick up the phone today and call someone you know would like to hear from you.

- ✔ Drop a line to a friend you haven't seen for some time.

- ✔ Get in touch with a member of your family who you haven't spoken to recently. Perhaps you've lost touch with an elderly relative, or maybe even a parent or sibling.

Consider using good old-fashioned pen and paper. Not many people write letters any more, and although the round-robin letter is a familiar method of updating friends at Christmas, nothing's to stop you from sending a personal card or letter to an older relative who may not have access to the latest technology. Now you've freed up more of your time, you can spend a few minutes writing a letter, while or instead of watching TV.

✔ Make a list of all your friends and family you're out of touch with and want to reconnect with and make an effort to contact at least one of them a week for the next few weeks.

# Making Time for Your Partner

When your partner is always there, you can often end up taking him or her for granted and not setting aside time to spend together.

How happy and content are you with your relationship as it is now? Perhaps you don't spend the amount of time with your partner that you'd like to, or the time that you do spend together is just part of the day-to-day routine. Is your relationship stuck in a rut without any fun?

Do you both know what you need and want from each other – do you have each other as a priority in your relationship?

Communication is important. Saying what you feel is central to maintaining a good relationship. Set aside time to talk to your partner on a regular basis when you won't be interrupted. Actively listen to what your partner is saying without jumping to any conclusions or interpreting according to your own perceptions.

Don't expect your partner to be a mind-reader and don't be surprised if he or she doesn't understand how you feel if you don't tell them. Make sure that you find time to talk to each other on a regular basis, so that communication doesn't become a problem between you.

In the hustle and bustle of a busy life, you may not find time for each other as you rush from home to work, catch up in a few quick moments over a meal in front of the TV, grab a few hours' sleep, and then head off to work again.

Follow these tips for making the time to spend with your partner:

- Go on a date with your partner every once in a while in addition to those birthdays and anniversaries. Book a meal at your partner's favourite restaurant, get tickets to the theatre, or go to a concert. Go for a picnic at the weekend, try a new activity together, take a trip to the beach. Alternatively, have a 'date' at home – spoil your partner with a favourite meal with candles and romantic music.

- Spend some quality time together doing something you both enjoy, when you won't be interrupted by children or the minutiae of everyday life.

- Get away together just as a couple and always set clear boundaries around adult time and space. Ask a friend or relative to baby-sit for you.

You don't need to go for grand gestures, simple things can often say so much more. The fact that you've put a little time and effort into something that shows you know what your partner enjoys – cooking a meal, planning a surprise, buying a gift – is enough.

Make a list (yep, another one!) of things you enjoy doing together and come up with some new ideas. Your list perhaps includes:

- Watching a film.

- Playing a board or card game.

- Going dancing.

- Having a special meal.

- Giving each other a massage, manicure, or pedicure.

- Visiting a museum or art gallery.

- Joining an evening class.

- Sport or an outdoor activity.

Don't be afraid to spend time apart too. Spending all your time together can be just as unhealthy as not spending enough time. You can still maintain separate interests as long as the balance is there. Then you've always got something to talk about as you tell your partner what you've been up to.

Make your relationship a priority. Plan in your schedule when you're going to spend time together. Plan in your dates and don't cancel.

# Part VI
## The Part of Tens

"It's just one meeting after another."

## In this part . . .

At certain times during the day you can find yourself with a few minutes to spare. Dip in here for ten ideas on how to make the most of that time. You'll also find a list of ten gadgets to save you even more time.

# Chapter 17

# Ten Ways to Be More Productive in Your Slack Time

*In This Chapter*

▶ Making the most of the unexpected minutes

▶ Finding quick moments of productivity

▶ Grabbing opportunities to clear out, catch up, and get creative

▶ Using quiet time to recharge and reenergise

*I*n the project management world, *slack time* is built into a project as a buffer, so that a certain task can overrun without impacting the next task or tasks. You can use the same strategy to build slack time into your own tasks, to give you a bit of leeway for when things go wrong.

At first glance, the words *slack time* may seem negative, describing unproductive wasted time when nothing happens. But in this chapter I turn that interpretation on its head and show you that slack time can be a useful time management opportunity, especially when you've already planned your time and know what you need to do.

You can use slack time to carve out a few bonus minutes in the day you didn't expect to have to yourself. You always have times when you find yourself twiddling your thumbs – whether you're waiting for a meeting, get delayed on a train, or find yourself arriving early for an appointment. Sometimes a cancelled meeting means you have a whole extra hour or longer that you hadn't planned for.

A spare five or ten minutes each day adds up to an extra hour a week – an hour you didn't know that you had. And the bits and pieces you can do in those few moments add up to big time-savings. Read on for just a few ideas of how you can fill those spare minutes, so that you don't ever need to feel that you're wasting your time.

# Being Prepared

As the Scout's motto says, 'Be prepared'. Take work with you and, as I recommend in Chapter 6, plan to arrive at meetings well ahead of time. Even if you're delayed, you'll still turn up on time, but if you do arrive early you've got some slack time in which to work.

I often take my laptop with me when I travel, so that if I arrive early I can sit and get on with some work without the usual interruptions I'd have if I was in the office. Sometimes a change of scene can increase your productivity by removing the distractions of your usual environment. (See Chapter 10 for tips on tackling interruptions and distractions.)

# Catching Up on Reading

Always carry something to read – a book, a magazine, a report, or your reading folder (refer to Chapter 7) containing articles and newsletters that you've put to one side for just such a quiet moment.

Pop a book into your laptop bag, briefcase, or handbag so that you have something to occupy you during odd bits of slack times. If you're anything like me, you've probably got a few books lying around at home waiting to be read. If the book is on a topic that relates to your work, it may trigger a few new ideas.

You can download many books in e-book format or on audio to laptops, PDAs, and MP3 players. This format can also be useful for business material, short documents, and reports that don't require a lot of concentration. But do remember that a small screen size limits the amount you can comfortably read.

Doctors' or dentists' waiting rooms can be a good place to catch up on your reading. You're nearly always kept waiting in these places. Rather than browsing the array of out-of-date gossip magazines, take your own with you and use the time to read something you actually want or need to read.

# Sorting Your Emails

Whether you're in front of your computer or out with your email-enabled PDA, just a few spare minutes can do wonders for your email management. If you get stuck on hold on the phone, or you only have ten minutes before your lunch appointment arrives, these provide ideal times to go through your emails, especially any reading or backlog ones. This is the exception to the rule of handling emails in blocks of time – treat this as a mini bonus block.

You can do some email spring-cleaning – binning unwanted emails; catching up with new emails in your inbox, and scanning any messages you put aside to read when you had time (you do now!). Flick to Chapter 8 for more timely ways to deal with emails.

# Managing Your Mobile

A few minutes spare is an ideal time to take on the little tasks that you wouldn't normally schedule the time for – such as doing some mobile admin.

Delete old text messages from your phone; they clog up the memory. Check through the address book on your phone and delete any old or redundant contacts (don't get too trigger-happy, though, or you may lose a valuable phone number). Finally, transfer numbers from your handset to the SIM card (the little card inside the phone that contains a data chip), so that you have a backup in case you drop, crush, or drown your mobile.

# Making Some Calls

One of the advantages of having a mobile phone is that you can communicate with someone while you're on the move (hands-free in the car, of course) away from home or the office. You can even plan time to make calls when you're travelling. Those spare moments when, in the past, you weren't contactable now come in useful – when it suits you.

If you organise your phone calls (see Chapter 9) not only do you know which calls you need to make that day but you already have the numbers you need with you.

So when you find yourself sitting waiting for a train or a delayed meeting, take a few minutes to make one of the calls that's on today's action list (Chapter 4 shows you how to make this list). Alternatively, catch up with a friend. You may catch him at a wrong moment but at least you've made contact rather than it being one of those calls you keep putting off until you have time.

# Taking Notes

Slack time can be creative and planning time. Let your mind idly wander and generate new, great ideas, or use a few spare minutes to do some planning. Jot down your ideas and plans in your notebook as they come to you.

Recording sudden inspiration is just one of the reasons why having a notebook with you at all times is great for productivity. You can also use spare moments to go over previous notes you've written, and remind yourself of progress you've made or things you still need to do.

My notebook includes mindmaps of seminars and workshops I've attended, notes from meetings, brain-storming sessions, action lists, planning notes, random jottings, and quotes. What you note down is entirely up to you. (Chapter 18 gives you more information about creating mind maps.)

# Resolving Two Issues with a Single Action

Combining is a great way to maximise your time – whether that's slack time waiting for a bus or for the toaster to pop up, or time spent on leisure activities or at work. *Combining* basically involves putting together two tasks in the same time slot.

Combining is something that we do quite naturally all the time; reading a book while commuting to work on the bus or train, walking and talking or these days, walking and texting! It's a technique you can use to get more done.

Here are some simple examples of combining:

- ✔ Dusting the lounge while watching TV.
- ✔ Washing up while waiting for the kettle to boil.
- ✔ Arranging two meetings in one trip, rather than driving the same distance on two different occasions.
- ✔ Walking or cycling to a meeting – fitting exercise in without making specific time to visit the gym or attend a class.
- ✔ Stopping off at the supermarket on your way back from a trip into town.

If you plan your time correctly, you're better able to see opportunities for combining more easily.

 Walking and talking is a great way to combine activities. If you need to get to a meeting and someone wants a few minutes of your time just as you're leaving the office – ask your colleague to walk with you.

 Combining isn't ideal when one of the tasks requires your attention or concentration (especially when driving). For example, watching a gripping thriller DVD while ironing may result in a scorched shirt (or worse, a nasty burn). Use common sense when choosing which activities you combine!

# Making Time for Fitness

People are always telling me that they simply can't find time to exercise. The simple solution is to think about being more active generally as well as building exercise into your slack time. Whether you have an extra ten minutes, half-an-hour, or longer, you have the opportunity to get in some form of activity.

Meeting cancelled? Why not use the time you've already blocked out for the meeting to get active – Chapter 15 has plenty of ideas.

Arrived early for a meeting? Take a walk round the area – at least you're not sitting doing nothing.

Got a meeting in London or any large city or town and you're in good time? Walk rather than take the bus or tube, or get off a few stops early and stroll the remaining distance. Stretching your legs wakes up your body and mind, and gives you the chance to mentally prepare for your meeting.

# Stretching Away Tension

When you get a few minutes spare try these simple, do any-where, tension-release stretches.

- ✔ Raise your arms above your head and link your hands together, palms facing outwards. Push your hands up towards the ceiling.

- ✔ Link your hands behind your back and press your palms away from you with your arms straight. Push your shoulders back and feel the stretch across your upper chest.

- ✔ Stretch your arms in front of you, link your hands with palms facing away from you. Stretch your shoulders forward and feel the stretch across the back of your shoulders.

- ✔ Shrug your shoulders towards your ears and hold. Do this while circling your shoulders forwards and back a few times.

- ✔ Hold your head upright and lean your head towards your shoulder feeling the stretch down the other side of your neck. Repeat on the other side.

> ✔ Raise one arm in the air and bend your elbow so that your hand goes behind your head, between your shoulder blades. Repeat on the other side.
>
> ✔ Put one arm behind your back, bend your elbow and reach your hand up your back as far you can go towards your shoulder blades. Repeat on the other side.
>
> ✔ Using your wrists, circle your hands in one direction a few times and then reverse. Do both hands at once.
>
> ✔ Gently draw a circle with your foot in one direction for a few circles and then the other.

# Taking It Easy

Take a break and re-energise. When you find yourself with a few minutes to spare, why not just relax and do nothing? After your rest, you'll feel calmer and more energetic, and you may find you're more efficient at tasks thanks to recharging those batteries.

If you're the sort of person that's constantly on the go, you may find it hard to unwind, but that in itself is probably a very good reason to do it. You might start twitching after ten minutes if you don't have something to occupy your hands or mind, but take the time to just chill. Chapter 15 has some simple breathing exercises that can help you let go and relax.

Don't feel that just because you have a busy action list you need to fill every spare minute with some form of activity. After all, you're probably also saying that you never get time for yourself. Everyone deserves a treat now and again (see Chapter 10 for more on the power of rewards).

# Chapter 18

# Ten Time-Saving Gadgets

*B*y their very nature gadgets are designed to save you time – lawnmowers make short work of taming unruly gardens, food processors dice onions in seconds, and the remote control saves you getting up from your cosy armchair to change the channel. And technology is advancing at a breathtaking pace – these days your mobile phone may contain a high-spec camera and the equivalent power of an early laptop!

In this chapter, I give you the low-down on some of the most useful time-saving gadgets for your collection. Of course, technology changes so rapidly that what's available now may be superseded in six months' time by something twice as powerful and probably half the price, so keep your eye on the market. Read product reviews and talk to friends and colleagues, to get their recommendations on the gadgets and tools that work for them.

All the gadgets I explore in this chapter are intended to save you time, not to become another source of distraction or to waste time. If you find that the gadget isn't saving you time, or is more hassle than it's worth, then ditch it. Just because you can use a gadget, doesn't mean you should.

# Audio Player

Listening to CDs, or MP3 files, provides a great way to absorb information in a different format. Car stereos, home music systems, computers, and personal devices – gadget-lovers have plenty of choice. You can listen to motivational CDs, audio books, a foreign language course, or downloads of your favourite radio programme that you missed.

And the beauty of an audio player is that it gives you the freedom to multitask – you can listen on a long car journey, while walking to work, or as you file paperwork. Even if your attention isn't 100 per cent focused on the audio (just as well, if you're driving!), you certainly hear the key points and repeated listening helps you understand the information even more.

For example, I listened to a whole series of CDs while travelling round the M25 on several journeys. The CDs accompanied a written course I was taking, so I received the same information in two different ways, which reinforced the content and meaning.

# Digital Voice Recorder

Everything is going digital these days and that applies to methods of recording too. Step aside the old-fashioned tape recorder and microphone, and enter the digital voice recorder, which records everything digitally into a small handheld device.

Digital recorders can be very useful for capturing thoughts and ideas while you're on the move – in the car (they can be voice activated), while commuting, or just when you're out and about. Index and organise your audio files into separate folders on the digital recorder to save time searching.

You can also use this gizmo to record meetings, seminars, workshops, and telephone calls (with the attendees' or caller's permission), or to capture notes for writing up later.

You can download audio files from the digital recorder to your computer and convert them to WAV, WAM, or MP3 format for playing on personal players. Some models also convert audio files into text documents using voice recognition and transcription software – saving you time having to type them out.

Carry a spare battery so you always have the maximum capacity for recording. Nothing is more frustrating than running out of juice just at the critical moment.

# Mobile Phone

Whatever did we do before we had mobile phones? These days people can contact you any time, anywhere – a situation that has its pros and cons.

On the positive side, in business, being able to contact people when you're not in the office, or outside of normal working hours, can be useful. And, of course, mobiles are essential if you're running late for a meeting or get caught up in traffic (although if you follow the tips in the rest of this book, hopefully this won't happen often).

But the less attractive side of mobile phones is feeling you can never get away from people contacting you. The simple answer? Remember that it's perfectly okay to switch your phone off sometimes!

# Notebook

Ah, the good old-fashioned pen and paper – not exactly a gadget but definitely a useful tool. Carry a notebook with you everywhere you go and use it to jot down:

- Ideas, thoughts, and notes for your weekly action list (see Chapter 4 for more on lists).
- Notes and mind maps in meetings (flick to Chapter 6 for meeting tips, and the nearby sidebar on mind maps).
- Contact details for people you meet.
- Sketches or outlines for projects.

Wherever you go make sure that you have one notebook with you, so you're never without something to write in. You never know when you'll need to write something down, and you don't want to end up with scraps of paper and lists all over the place.

## Mind maps: Notes with a difference

Mind maps are a visual representation of ideas, tasks, or notes on a single sheet of paper. Based around a central idea or theme, the connecting thoughts or information branch off from the centre. You use colour, single words, and images rather than long sentences. You can use them to summarise information, solve problems, and create structure. Have a go at creating a mind map:

✔ Write a word or draw an image to represent the main subject in the centre of the paper.

✔ Draw branches from this central word or image to represent different but related topics or sub-headings. Use colour if you like.

✔ Label each branch and add further branches for each additional piece of information – words, images, and symbols. Add in new links and branches as you think of them.

Whereas most maps are easily drawn by hand, software applications such as Mindjet and MindManager exist to create mind maps on your computer.

To see some examples of mind maps have a look at the website of mind map guru Tony Buzan at `www.buzanworld.com/mindmaps`.

By keeping your notebook up to date you always know where that important piece of information is. And as part of your daily planning, and when you have a few spare minutes, you can go through and review what you've written previously.

You can also use your notebook as a journal. Many people like to keep a regular diary of events – who they've met, what they've done, what they'd like to do. *Journalling* is a way of clarifying your thoughts and ideas, and can help with setting goals and solving problems. Getting everything down on paper is better than trying to keep it all your head.

## *Personal Organiser or PDA*

An electronic personal organiser, or personal digital assistant (PDA), is essentially a small hand-held device that stores your calendar, address book, and notes. The gadget also acts as a clock, calculator, and mini-computer.

The earliest models were rather heavy and clunky but, as with all technology, PDAs have become smaller and more powerful over time. These days they're no bigger than a phone and also include email, Internet access, phone, and a music player, so you can have everything you need on the move. Many mobile phones now also function as a PDA.

The beauty of PDAs is that they come with software that synchronises with applications such as Microsoft Outlook on your computer – using the USB port, a separate cable, or Bluetooth (see the sidebar 'Avoiding the Bluetooth blues').

PDAs are great if you don't want to take your laptop with you. When you get back to the office you just upload the new information you've entered.

Having synchronised with your computer, you can quickly recover the data if the battery goes flat or your device is lost or stolen.

Hundreds of third-party applications are available for PDAs that allow you to personalise them for your use. Use your PDA to log your times when jogging, calculate exchange rates, navigate (with the Global Positioning System, or GPS), read e-books, track your expenses on a spreadsheet, or use it as a dictionary or word processor.

## Avoiding the Bluetooth blues

Bluetooth is a wireless technology that connects devices like PDAs, mobile phones, cameras, laptops, printers, and many other peripheral devices over short distances. Any Bluetooth-enabled device that's within range can connect with another bluetooth device to exchange data and information.

Be careful when using Bluetooth on your PDA or mobile phone. If you don't set the connection preferences correctly, your device may automatically connect to others, which means someone can access your device (and information) without your knowledge.

Make sure that you check your settings carefully before taking advantage of Bluetooth's time-saving capabilities.

Make sure that you recharge and resynchronise your PDA every time you get back to the office or back home. That way your calendar is always up to date, and you don't risk losing all your data thanks to a flat battery.

# Sat Nav

If you travel a lot as part of your work then Sat Nav (Satellite Navigation System) may be an essential tool to save you time when driving. Sat Navs are small devices with a screen and touch keys that sit on the dashboard of your car and work out where you are by receiving signals from satellites.

You enter your starting point and destination and it works out the route, giving you directions by voice, symbols or on-screen maps. Some maps also show you local facilities such as petrol stations, banks, cafés, restaurants, and points of interest. If you take a wrong turn it automatically works out your new route to get you back on track and save you time getting lost. To get on with your Sat Nav you need to cope with listening to verbal instructions as you drive.

Some systems are better than others, and no Sat Nav is infallible, but these gizmos can certainly save you time getting to your destination. If you're stuck in traffic or delayed by an accident up ahead you can quickly choose a new route without having to pull over and work it out on a map.

Don't rely 100 per cent on your Sat Nav. You should always have at least an idea of where you're going so that if it all goes wrong you're not totally lost or end up down some track in the country.

# Scanner

A scanner is a device that enables you to scan documents and images and store them on your computer. You can then easily send images from your computer or store the data in electronic format. Plug the scanner into the USB port on your computer and upload files straight into your applications, such as Microsoft Word, Excel, Outlook, or Adobe Photoshop. OCR (Optical Character Recognition) software comes with most scanners and enables scanned pages to be converted into editable text without having to spend time retyping them.

You may find the following types of scanner useful:

- ✔ **Business card scanner.** If you regularly go to meetings where you exchange business cards, then it's likely you have a stack of business cards at home. A business card scanner saves you entering all the contact's details when you get home. You simply scan the card and then you can synchronise with your contact system – such as Outlook – or with your PDA or mobile phone.

- ✔ **Document scanner.** These days scanners aren't necessarily big hefty machines the size of a printer – some are small enough to be handheld devices. You can even find one the size of a pen (a large chunky pen) that enables you to scan documents, photos, contracts, and forms while you're on the move.

- ✔ **Combined Printer/Scanner.** Scanning functions are also included with some models of desktop printers to save having two devices taking up space in your office.

# Telephone Headset

Headsets are superb for multitasking, allowing you to chat on the phone with both hands free to do other tasks. You plug the headset directly into the headset connection on the phone, or connect via wireless or Bluetooth technology, and away you go.

Unhindered by the cumbersome telephone (and its entangling cord), you're free to get on with any number of jobs. If you use the headset for work, not only are your hands free to use the computer or write notes while you're on the phone, but you can also multitask in other ways – organising files or reaching for a book you need while avoiding a crick in your neck from the phone tucked under your chin.

At home, using a headset leaves your hands free to tidy up, sort the post, or wander into another room to fetch something while you chat. And if a friend phones up when you're preparing dinner in the kitchen, rather than interrupt your timings, you can chat as you chop, mix, fry, boil, and bake.

# Timer

A timer is one of the simplest time-saving gadgets you can get hold of. You can use a timer to limit your distractions and keep you focused. When the clock is running you're more efficient, more focused, and less distracted.

It doesn't matter whether you use a manual, wind-up kitchen timer, or a digital timer. Manual timers usually allow you to set the time in minutes up to one hour. Digital timers enable you to set the time for up to 99 minutes and to the second and can be set to count down or up. They can also act as a stopwatch so you can monitor how long you spend on a particular task.

Setting an hourly alarm on your phone, computer, or watch reminds you of the passage of time and pulls you back on track if you get diverted. Refer to Chapter 10 for more on the benefits of setting alarms.

# USB Flash Drive

Also known as memory sticks, thumbnail, or pen drives, these tiny removable data-storage devices are readily available from all good computer stores and great for saving stuff from your computer. They come in various sizes that have the capacity to save anything from a few documents up to hundreds of files. All you do is plug the stick into the USB port on your computer, and then transfer files across to the new drive.

Pop your latest files on a Flash Drive when you want to transfer data between the office and the home, share files with someone else or when you visit a client. You can also use this as an alternative way of backing up your important documents (see Chapter 7 for more on backups).

Memory sticks are also used in digital cameras and PDAs. By plugging in the stick, you extend the number of photos and files you can store. Take a spare stick for your camera if you're going on holiday.

# Index

# Notes

# Notes

# Notes

# Notes

# Notes

# Notes

# FOR DUMMIES®

## Do Anything. Just Add Dummies

---

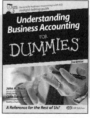

# FOR DUMMIES®

## The easy way to get more done and have more fun

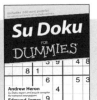
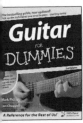
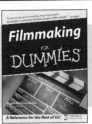

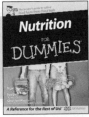
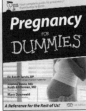